Julie Stafford's
TASTE OF LIFE
Family
COOKBOOK

By the same author

Taste of Life
Taste of Life from the Microwave
Julie Stafford's Low Cholesterol Cookbook
Julie Stafford's Juicing for Health
Julie Stafford's Muffin Book
Julie Stafford's Wok Cookbook

Julie Stafford's

TASTE OF LIFE

Family
COOKBOOK

VIKING

Viking
Penguin Books Australia Ltd
487 Maroondah Highway, PO Box 257
Ringwood, Victoria 3134, Australia
Penguin Books Ltd
Harmondsworth, Middlesex, England
Viking Penguin, A Division of Penguin Books USA Inc.
375 Hudson Street, New York, New York 10014, USA
Penguin Books Canada Limited
10 Alcorn Avenue, Toronto, Ontario, Canada M4V 3B2
Penguin Books (N.Z.) Ltd
Cnr Rosedale and Airborne Roads, Albany, Auckland, New Zealand

First published by Penguin Books Australia Ltd 1990
This edition published 1997

10 9 8 7 6 5 4 3 2 1

Photography by Mark Chew
Food preparation and styling by Fiona Hammond
Illustrations by Cathy Larsen
Typeset in 10/15pt Goudy by Midland Typesetters
Printed in Australia by Australian Print Group, Maryborough, Victoria

National Library of Australia
Cataloguing-in-Publication data

Stafford, Julie.
    Julie Stafford's taste of life family cookbook.

    {New ed.}.
    Includes index.
    ISBN 0 670 87576 7.

    1. Cookery (Natural foods). I. Title. II. Title: Taste of life family cookbook.

641.5637

Front cover photograph
Spinach and Cottage Cheese
Cannelloni (see page 74).

CONTENTS

INTRODUCTION

We now recognise the importance of having *all* family members conscious of the foods they eat. Health problems associated with poor dietary habits do not start at the age of forty: they begin at childhood, when our eating patterns are formed. If we grow up eating all the wrong types of foods, we place ourselves at a high risk of developing heart disease, cancer, adult diabetes and obesity in later years, and generally having a poor state of health. If, on the other hand, we eat a balanced, nutritious diet most of the time, we are at least living in a way that will prevent the onset of many of today's common diseases.

However, eating well does not mean eating tasteless or boring foods. My *Taste of Life Family Cookbook* provides recipes for the whole family to enjoy together, recipes containing delicious low-cholesterol, low-fat, low-sugar, low-salt and high-fibre nutritious foods.

STOCKING THE PANTRY

agar   This is a seaweed-based setting agent like gelatine. It is high in protein and calcium and easy to digest. In this book granulated agar powder is almost always used. One teaspoon of agar sets approximately one cup of liquid, depending on the texture you require.

almonds   These are the only nuts used in the recipes. Almonds contain polyunsaturated fats and are a high-quality, nutritious food. However, to reduce fat intake in the diet it is important to keep recipes containing almonds to a minimum. Use those recipes for special occasions. Almonds are best bought in their shells and shelled as required. Unshelled nuts are protected from heat, air, light and moisture and will keep almost indefinitely.

apple juice concentrate   This is apple juice boiled down to a syrup. It can be reconstituted to an apple juice drink by adding water. 'Apple juice is preferred to honey because it contains vitamins, minerals and water-soluble fibre (pectin) which honey does not have. Honey is approximately 80 per cent sugar and apple juice concentrate is approximately 66 per cent. Honey has 61 calories per tablespoon and apple juice concentrate has 30 calories per tablespoon.' (Nutrition Department, Pritikin Longevity Center.)

baking powder (sodium-free)   All recipes in this book using flour and baking powder use commercially packaged baking powder. To maintain a diet low in sodium you can make your own sodium-free baking powder by using equal quantities – say, two tablespoons each – of cornflour, cream of tartar and potassium bi-carbonate (available at chemists). Sift ingredients together and store in an airtight jar.

Shake before using. Use approximately two teaspoons of this baking powder for every one cup of flour. The baking powder will begin to react once it combines with moisture so you need to work quickly at this stage, placing it in the oven before it subsides. (A better result in your baking of cakes may be achieved by increasing oven temperature by 5°C and reducing cooking time by 5 minutes.)

brown rice   Brown rice is the natural, unpolished rice that has been hulled but still has its bran. The bran in brown rice offers additional protein, plus traces of iron, calcium and vitamin B. It has a nutty flavour and is extremely nutritious. It takes longer to cook than white rice.

canned and packaged foods   Use canned and packaged foods only when fresh food is not available or is too expensive. Become a label reader! Look for natural food, without sugar, salt or other additives. It is one thing to save a few cents on an item containing lots of additives, but later in life that saving can become a burden.

Caro   This is a cereal beverage made of roasted, malted barley, barley, chicory and rye. For children who like a 'hot cuppa' with mum and dad, it is an excellent choice. It is caffeine-free.

carob   This is a fine dark powder. It comes from carob pods (from carob trees) which are deseeded, toasted and ground to made a sweet-tasting flavouring agent. Add to cakes and treats, drinks and desserts. Use slightly more carob in recipes when substituting it for cocoa. Carob contains natural sugar. It is caffeine-free, so it is preferable to chocolate or cocoa.

chicken stock   Boil up some chicken carcasses and/or meat in a combination of water and orange juice. Add onion, celery and carrot, and ginger root or garlic. Let simmer for two hours. Strain, cool and defat. Use as required.

cold pressed oil   When oil is extracted with little or no heat – or with the use of chemical solvents, as happens with ordinary oils – the vitamin E content is not destroyed. Oil should be bought in brown bottles or tins, kept away from light and refrigerated. Do not use oil excessively and only in the amounts given in the recipes. I use almond oil for sweet cooking or grapeseed oil, and use recipes containing oil in moderation.

dried fruits   These include apricots, apples, raisins, sultanas, currants, bananas, peaches, nectarines and pears. Dried fruits contain a high level of natural sugar, so they should not be eaten in excess. Look for sun-dried fruits without additives where possible.

eggs   Egg whites are used in a number of recipes to reduce fat and cholesterol. The egg white protein, when whipped to form stiff peaks, breaks down into short strands and these expand, forming elastic-walled cells that trap air. The cells in turn expand when heated. This is what makes egg whites such a valuable raising agent. Yolk protein, on the other hand, binds and thickens. It can be substituted by doubling the egg whites for the number of eggs in a recipe or by adding a small amount of another thickening and binding ingredient like arrowroot, grated or cooked apple or fresh banana. All recipes that call for eggs use 55 g eggs.

evaporated low-fat milk   This is canned milk with a large percentage of water removed. It contains no sugar, has a heavier texture than non-fat milk, and is a good substitute in recipes calling for whole milk. It is 'pure skim milk with 60 per cent of water removed and contains less than ½ per cent fat'.

fruit juices   The best quality juices are obtained by juicing fresh fruits and vegetables and returning fruit fibre to the liquid. When buying fruit juices choose those that do not have sugar added to them and are preservative-free. Do not overuse juices. Encourage children to drink plenty of water from an early age.

garlic   This is a bulbous plant of the onion family. The bulb is composed of many small cloves enclosed in papery skins. It has a long history of uses, both culinary and medicinal, and is said to be one of nature's most effective natural antibiotics. It has a very pungent flavour and enhances many dishes.

ginger   Peel the root before chopping up very finely. To make fresh ginger juice, place small pieces in a garlic crusher and squeeze. It is used to flavour many dishes, spicy and sweet. It is also reputed to be an excellent remedy for sore throats and stomach upsets.

herb teas   There is much nutritional value in herb teas. The whole family will enjoy them chilled with ice blocks and slices of lemon or lime.

herbs   These are best grown fresh in your garden, but you should also explore and decide which dried varieties suit your palate. These can be used individually or combined to create wonderful flavours in sweet or spicy recipes, without the need to add salt or sugar.

low-fat ricotta cheese   This is made from the curd rather than the liquid milk, which is drained off. It has a bland flavour and is a mass of fine, small curd particles. It is suitable to add to savoury or sweet dishes and is delicious just as it is on vegetable crudités, wholemeal bread or wholemeal biscuits. Preferably look for cheese with 1 per cent fat content.

Natex   This is a low-salt yeast extract which is similar in taste and appearance to Vegemite. It contains no artificial additives or preservatives. Use on toast or in sandwiches.

non-fat buttermilk   Originally buttermilk was the liquid drained from the churn after butter-making. Today buttermilk is made by adding selected bacteria to non-fat milk. It is slightly acidic in flavour, thicker in consistency than milk, and thinner than yoghurt. Nutritionally it compares with skim milk, with a maximum fat content of around 0.8 per cent. Buttermilk can be substituted for milk in any recipe.

non-fat cottage cheese   This cheese has the consistency of paste and has a light acidic flavour, though it is still fairly bland. It contains a maximum of about 0.4 per cent fat. Again, it is suitable for savoury or sweet dishes.

low-fat milk   This is milk with less than 1 per cent milk fat. It still contains the nutrients of whole milk except for fat-soluble vitamins.

non-fat yoghurt   This is a cultured milk product. Specific bacteria are added to fresh skim milk to develop a tangy flavoured, custard-like yoghurt. It is more nutritious than milk because an extra 4 per cent of non-fat milk powder is added to enhance the texture. It has a fat content of approximately 0.1 per cent.

orange and lemon essences   These are concentrated extracts of the fruits. Use pure essences and use them sparingly.

peppermint essence This is a concentrated oil from the steamed distillation of the peppermint plant.

pinenuts, sunflower seeds, poppy seeds, pumpkin kernels and sesame seeds These are used very sparingly to flavour some recipes. All can be bought at health food shops.

shredded coconut Coconut is an excellent source of phosphorus and potassium but is high in polyunsaturated fat. A small amount is occasionally called for to flavour a recipe, but use sparingly.

skim milk powder This is milk from which the moisture and fat has been removed. It is added to dry ingredients in baking or reconstituted by adding water.

soy sauce A dark, almost black, thin sauce made from fermented soy beans. It enhances vegetable, meat and rice dishes. Use only a low-salt variety.

sprouts Alfalfa sprouts are the most common, but mung beans and lentils are also excellent sprouted. Buy ready sprouted or sprout your own. Alfalfa sprouts are rich in nearly all vitamins and minerals. They are a good source of protein and enzymes, as are most other sprouts.

tofu This is soy bean curd. It is made by adding a natural coagulant (lemon juice) to soy milk. Curds are created, the excess milk drained off and the curds pressed into blocks to remove all liquid. It has an excellent protein and calcium content, is low in fat and is cholesterol free. Tofu has a bland taste and can be used for salads, sweet or savoury dishes.

tomato paste This is a concentrated purée of tomatoes. You can make your own tomato paste by peeling and deseeding very ripe tomatoes. Chop them up finely and cook until they thicken. Do not add any liquid. Alternatively, you can use low-salt commercial varieties.

unbleached white flour This is wholemeal flour with the bran and husks removed, but without the addition of chemicals. Use in conjunction with wholemeal flour to increase the fibre value of the recipe.

unbleached wholemeal flour One-hundred-per-cent wholemeal flour has the highest nutrient and protein value, as well as bran for essential fibre.

vanilla essence   The pure vanilla essence is obtained by steeping the vanilla pods in alcohol (usually brandy) and water over a period of time.

Vecon   This is concentrated vegetable stock with vitamins. It makes a quick vegetable stock when reconstituted with water. The amount will be determined by the flavour required. Add it to casseroles, soups and gravies when a suitable stock is not available.

vegetable stock   Combine mixed vegetables and spices, cover with water and simmer for 2 hours. Strain and cool.

wholemeal bread   Choose varieties that are salt-free or low in salt, sugar-free and oil-free or low in oil. Those breads containing grains are an excellent choice. Introduce variations in bread types such as rye bread and sourdough. Making your own bread is one sure way of knowing what actually goes into it.

filo pastry   This is excellent for wrapping food and it contains no fat. Dry bake in the oven until filling is cooked and pastry is crisp. Because it is paper-thin you will need several sheets of pastry to make a layer for the base of a pie.

wholemeal pita bread   Also known as flatbread or Lebanese bread, it is basically made from wholemeal flour, water and minimal salt. It is excellent just as it is, or open one end and fill with salad ingredients. It also makes an excellent pizza base.

yeast   Baker's yeast in granulated form is used in all recipes to act as a leavener for breads and pizza dough.

MEASUREMENTS AND OVEN TEMPERATURES

Measurements

1 metric cup = 250 ml

1 tablespoon = 20 ml

1 teaspoon = 5 ml

Spoon measures are level measurements.

Oven Temperatures

SLOW OVEN

150–170°C (300–350°F)

MODERATE OVEN

170–190°C (350–375°F)

HOT OVEN

200°C (400°F)

VERY HOT OVEN

220–240°C (425–450°F)

Conversions and substitutes

¼ teaspoon dried herbs = 2 teaspoons fresh herbs

....

2 cloves fresh garlic, crushed = 1 teaspoon powdered garlic

....

4 teaspoons dry yeast = 30 g fresh yeast

....

1 cup carob powder = ¾ cup cocoa powder

....

2½ medium lemons = ½ cup lemon juice

....

1 medium onion = approximately 100 g

....

1 teaspoon agar powder sets approximately 1¼–2 cups of liquid, depending on setting consistency required

1 cm × 26 cm agar bar sets approximately 3 cups of liquid

....

1 cup uncooked brown rice = nearly 3 cups cooked brown rice

....

2 cups uncooked soyaroni noodles = 3 cups cooked noodles

....

1 cup skim milk powder = 4 cups liquid milk

....

1 cup wholemeal flour = approximately 150 g

....

1 cup rolled oats = approximately 150 g

....

1 cup whole almonds = approximately 150 g

BREAKFASTS

FRUIT AND VEGETABLE JUICES

Fresh squeezed or extracted fruit and vegetable juices are the most delicious and nutritious drinks. Some fruits and vegetables that cannot be squeezed can be placed in a juice extractor, which extracts the juice from the pulp by a rotary crushing action.

The pulp remaining is mainly fruit fibre and can be added to the juice for complete food value. Fruit pulp can also be added to cakes for extra moisture, or vegetable pulp to soups for added flavour. However, do not store the pulp. It loses its colour, taste and nutritional value.

Some juicing combinations
- Orange and pineapple.
- Orange and grapefruit.
- Apple and carrot.
- Apple and celery.
- Tomato and cucumber.

YUMMY HOME-MADE MUESLI

Makes approximately 1½ kg

1 cup wheatgerm
1 cup buckwheat
2 cups All Bran
4 cups rolled oats
½ cup sunflower seeds
1 cup almonds
½ cup dates, chopped
½ cup dried pineapple pieces
½ cup dried papaw pieces
½ cup dried apricots, chopped

Combine all ingredients and keep in an airtight container. Serve with low-fat milk.

RICE AND APPLE

Serves 1

½ cup uncooked brown rice
1 Granny Smith apple (other suitable
   cooking fruits can be substituted,
   i.e. pear, apricot, peach)
½ cup unsweetened orange juice
1½ cups water

Combine all ingredients in a saucepan.
Cover and simmer until all liquid is
absorbed and rice cooked (about
40 minutes).

The rice can be cooked the night
before if required and reheated in a
microwave oven the next morning, or
it can be eaten cold. It can also be
served with a little low-fat milk.

OAT BRAN PORRIDGE

Serves 1

⅓ cup oat bran
1 cup water

Slowly bring to the boil in a saucepan,
stirring continuously. Turn heat down,
cover and cook until it reaches desired
consistency.

(Oat bran porridge contains more bran
than traditional porridge.)

OAT BRAN AND OATMEAL PORRIDGE

Serves 1

¼ cup rolled oats
2 tablespoons oat bran
1 cup water

Slowly bring to the boil in a saucepan,
stirring continuously. Turn heat down,
cover and cook until it reaches desired
consistency.

CREAMY MILLET

Serves 2
1 cup millet
3 cups boiling water
1 apple, peeled and grated
pinch of cinnamon

Add millet to boiling water and stir briskly. Add apple and cinnamon. Turn heat down low and cover. Stir occasionally so millet does not stick to saucepan. Millet is cooked when it becomes creamy and loses its gritty texture.

APPLE SPREAD

Makes approximately 3½ cups
220 g dried apples
3 cups unsweetened pineapple juice
½ lemon
2 teaspoons grated lemon rind
2 teaspoons cinnamon

Combine all ingredients in a large saucepan and simmer over a gentle heat until apples are soft. Remove lemon. Purée the mixture in a blender and pour into sterilised jars. When cool, seal and store in the refrigerator.

CLEAR MARMALADE

Makes approximately 1¼ cups
1½ cups clear apple and pear juice
2 teaspoons apple juice concentrate
1 teaspoon agar powder
1 teaspoon finely grated lemon rind

Place all ingredients in a saucepan. Slowly bring to the boil, stirring to dissolve agar. As mixture comes to boil, turn down to simmer. Simmer for five minutes. Remove from heat and pour into sterilised jar. As mixture begins to set, stir with a spoon to keep the lemon rind evenly distributed through the spread. Cool and refrigerate.

BLUEBERRY JAM SPREAD

Makes approximately 3 cups
1½ cups unsweetened natural pear
   juice
⅓ cup apple juice concentrate
1 tablespoon lemon juice
2 teaspoons agar powder
450 g blueberries

Combine pear juice, apple juice
concentrate, lemon juice and agar in a
saucepan. Slowly bring to the boil,
stirring to dissolve the agar. Boil for
5 minutes. Add blueberries and boil
for another 10 minutes. Pour into
sterilised jars. Keep refrigerated.

APRICOT FRUIT SPREAD

Makes approximately 3½ cups
125 g dried apricots
90 g dried apples
60 g raisins
3½ cups unsweetened orange juice

Combine all ingredients in a large
saucepan and simmer over a gentle
heat until fruit is soft. Purée the
mixture in a blender and pour into
sterilised jars. When cool, seal and
store in the refrigerator.

CHERRY SPREAD

Makes approximately 3 cups
1 cup unsweetened orange juice
1 cup apple juice concentrate
1 tablespoon lemon juice
¼ teaspoon grated lemon rind
½ bar agar (cut into small pieces) or
   2 teaspoons agar powder
500 g stoned cherries

Place everything except the cherries in
a saucepan. Slowly bring to the boil.
Simmer for fifteen minutes, stirring
occasionally. Add cherries. Slowly
bring to the boil again. Simmer for
five minutes. Pour into sterilised jars.
Cool and refrigerate.

RASPBERRY SPREAD

Makes approximately 3½ cups
1¼ cups clear apple and pear juice
2 teaspoons agar powder
¼ cup apple juice concentrate
450 g raspberries

Place apple and pear juice, agar and
apple juice concentrate in a saucepan.
Slowly bring to the boil. Simmer for
5 minutes. Add raspberries. Slowly
bring to the boil again. Simmer for
5 minutes. Remove from heat. Pour
into sterilised jars. Cool and refrigerate.

STRAWBERRY SPREAD

Makes approximately 6 cups
2 cups unsweetened apple and pear
   juice or 2 cups unsweetened orange
   juice
4 teaspoons agar powder
¾ cup apple juice concentrate
1 kg strawberries

Place everything except the
strawberries in a saucepan and slowly
bring to the boil. Simmer for five
minutes. Add strawberries. Bring to
the boil again. Simmer for 20–25
minutes. Remove from heat. Pour into
sterilised jars. Cool and refrigerate.

OAT PANCAKES

Makes 6
1 cup rolled oats
½ cup oat bran
1 cup unbleached wholemeal plain
   flour
2 teaspoons baking powder
¼ cup apple juice concentrate
2 cups water or low-fat milk or
   low-fat soy milk
1 teaspoon vanilla essence
2 egg whites

In a large bowl combine rolled oats
and bran. Combine flour and baking
powder and sift over oats, returning
husks to mixture. Combine the next
three ingredients and stir through the
oat and flour mixture. Beat egg whites
until stiff and gently fold through
mixture. Cook in a lightly greased
non-stick pancake pan until browned
on both sides.

BUCKWHEAT, ORANGE AND OAT BRAN PANCAKES

Makes 6
¾ cup buckwheat flour
¾ cup oat bran
1 teaspoon baking powder
1 cup low-fat milk or low-fat soy
  milk
½ cup unsweetened orange juice
1 tablespoon apple juice concentrate
grated rind of 1 orange
2 egg whites

Combine all ingredients in a food processor. Purée until smooth. Pour a little mixture onto a hot pancake pan. Cook until both sides are brown.

CORNMEAL AND OAT BRAN PANCAKES

Makes 6
1 cup cornmeal (fine)
½ cup oat bran
2 teaspoons baking powder
1 tablespoon cold pressed oil
2 tablespoons apple juice concentrate
2 teaspoons vanilla essence
2 cups low-fat milk or low-fat soy
  milk
4 egg whites

Combine the first three ingredients and mix well. Combine the next four ingredients and stir into the cornmeal and oat mixture. Beat egg whites until stiff and gently fold through. Stand for ten minutes, then mix well again. Spoon onto a lightly greased non-stick pancake pan, cook until brown on both sides. Stir mixture well between each pancake. Excellent served with fresh bananas and lemon topping.

CHERRY PANCAKE TOPPING

1 cup unsweetened orange juice
½ cup apple juice concentrate
½ teaspoon orange essence
grated rind of 1 lemon
1 tablespoon lemon juice
1 teaspoon (scant) agar powder
500 g stoned cherries

Place all ingredients except cherries in a saucepan. Bring to the boil and simmer for 10–15 minutes. Add cherries and cook a further 5 minutes. Remove from heat and cool slightly. The mixture will become jelly-like in texture as it cools. Pour over pancakes.

BLUEBERRY PANCAKE TOPPING

2 cups unsweetened natural pear juice
¼ cup cornflour
⅓ cup apple juice concentrate
450 g blueberries, fresh or frozen
1 tablespoon lemon juice

Mix ¼ cup pear juice with cornflour to make a paste. Combine other ingredients in a small saucepan and slowly bring to the boil. Add cornflour and stir continuously until sauce thickens. Remove from heat and cool slightly. Pour over pancakes.

LEMON PANCAKE TOPPING

¾ cup lemon juice
½ cup apple juice concentrate
½ teaspoon orange essence
grated rind of 1 orange (optional)
1¼ cups water
¼ cup cornflour

Combine first 4 ingredients plus 1 cup of water in a small saucepan. Combine ¼ cup water and cornflour to make a paste. Slowly bring lemon mixture to the boil. Add cornflour mixture and stir continuously until sauce thickens. Remove from heat and cool slightly. Pour over pancakes.

BANANA PANCAKE TOPPING

1 banana (per pancake)
1½ cups unsweetened orange, pear or apple juice
1 tablespoon lemon juice
1 tablespoon apple juice concentrate
1–2 teaspoons cornflour

Add a little juice to cornflour to make a paste. Add remaining liquid to a pan and bring to the boil. Turn heat down and simmer until liquid reduces slightly. Slice bananas and add to the sauce. Bring to the boil and cook for 1 minute. Add cornflour and stir until sauce boils and thickens. Pour over pancakes.

APRICOT FRUIT SMOOTHIE

Serves 2

1 cup low-fat milk or low-fat soy
   milk, or goat's milk, ice-cold
½ cup fresh apricots, finely chopped
   or natural sugar-free canned
   apricots
2 ice blocks
1 teaspoon apple juice concentrate
¼ teaspoon cinnamon (optional)
2 tablespoons low-fat ricotta cheese
   (optional)

Place all ingredients in a food blender
or processor and blend until thick and
creamy. Add 2 tablespoons low-fat
ricotta cheese for a richer, creamier
smoothie.

APRICOT AND ALMOND SMOOTHIE

Serves 1

½ cup low-fat milk or low-fat soy
   milk, well chilled
½ cup unsweetened apple juice, well
   chilled
4 dried apricots, soaked and drained
5 almonds

Combine all ingredients in a food
blender or processor and blend until
thick and frothy.

BANANA FRUIT SMOOTHIE

Serves 1
1 small ripe banana (can be frozen)
1 cup low-fat milk or low-fat soy
  milk
½ teaspoon vanilla essence
4 ice blocks
dash of nutmeg (optional)

Chop banana roughly. Place all ingredients in a food blender or processor. Blend until smooth and frothy. The smoothie will be frothier and creamy smooth if you use frozen bananas.

You can make this smoothie into a Banana Creamy by substituting 1 cup of non-fat yoghurt for the low-fat milk.

BERRY FRUIT SMOOTHIE

Serves 2
1 cup low-fat milk or low-fat soy
  milk, well chilled
¼ cup non-fat yoghurt, well chilled
1 cup mixed berries (blueberries,
  strawberries, raspberries, etc.)
1 teaspoon apple juice concentrate

Combine all ingredients in a food blender or processor and blend until thick and frothy.

CAROB SMOOTHIE

Serves 2
1 cup low-fat milk or low-fat soy
  milk, well chilled
2 tablespoons skim milk powder
1 tablespoon carob powder
1 teaspoon vanilla essence
½ banana, chopped (optional)
nutmeg (for garnish)

Place all ingredients except nutmeg in a food blender or processor and blend until smooth and frothy. Pour into a tall glass full of ice blocks. Garnish with a sprinkle of nutmeg.

HONEY AND ALMOND SMOOTHIE

Serves 1

¾ cup low-fat milk or low-fat soy
milk, well chilled

5 almonds

1 teaspoon honey

2 teaspoons wheatgerm

Combine all ingredients in a food blender or processor and blend until thick and frothy.

STRAWBERRY SMOOTHIE

Serves 2

1 cup strawberries

2 tablespoons unsweetened orange
juice

1 tablespoon apple juice concentrate

2 cups low-fat milk or low-fat soy
milk, ice-cold

½ cup non-fat yoghurt

In a small saucepan simmer strawberries in orange juice and apple juice concentrate until strawberries are soft. Cool. Purée all ingredients and serve.

Variation

• Substitute 2 tablespoons skim milk
  powder for the non-fat yoghurt.

SOUPS

CHICKEN BROTH

Makes approximately 1 litre

3 kg chicken meat and bones or
   carcasses
1 teaspoon chopped garlic
2 teaspoons chopped fresh ginger
6 black peppercorns
1 large carrot
1 small parsnip
2 sticks celery
1 litre water

Put all the ingredients in a large
saucepan. Bring to the boil. Simmer
for at least 1 hour. Strain. Cool and
discard congealed fat before using.

For added flavour, add finely chopped
spring onions or finely chopped fresh
parsley and finely grated lemon rind.

VEGETABLE BROTH

Makes 3 litres

4½ litres water
half bunch celery (use the part with
   green leaves)
2 large brown onions
2 large carrots
good handful fresh parsley
1 tablespoon pink peppercorns

Combine water and celery in a
saucepan. Top and tail onions and
wash any dirt off skins. Cut in half,
add the onion (skin also) to the pot
with remaining ingredients. Bring to
the boil. Turn down and simmer for
2½–3 hours. Strain through a fine
sieve.

This is a very clear liquid full of
goodness and flavour which is
excellent served as a clear broth with
finely chopped fresh herbs; or grate
some vegetables and add to the stock,
bringing to the boil so vegetables are
just cooked.

The broth can also be used as a
vegetable stock to enhance the flavour
and be the base of other soups.

HEARTY VEGETABLE SOUP

Serves 8

8½ cups chicken stock or vegetable
  stock
1 small leek
1 cup chopped celery
1 cup chopped green beans
1 cup peas
2 cups chopped carrot
1 cup chopped zucchini or baby
  squash
1 cup chopped parsnip
¼ cup cracked wheat or barley
1 cup water or tomato juice
1 teaspoon dried marjoram
black pepper to taste
2 tablespoons chopped fresh herbs
  (parsley, thyme, chives, basil,
  oregano)

Combine all ingredients in a large pan
and gently simmer for 2 hours. Stir
occasionally so vegetables do not stick
to the bottom of the pan. Serve with
hot and crusty wholemeal bread to
make a meal.

CREAMY CAULIFLOWER SOUP

Serves 4–6

1 teaspoon crushed garlic
1 small leek or onion, chopped
1 teaspoon light olive oil (optional
  but creates an excellent flavour,
  substitute 1 teaspoon water if
  desired)
400 g cauliflower, chopped
200 g potato, peeled and chopped
4 cups vegetable broth or strained
  chicken broth (see page 14)
250 ml low-fat evaporated milk

Sauté garlic and leek or onion in the
oil over a very gentle heat until leek
or onion is soft. Add all other
ingredients and simmer until
vegetables are soft. Purée. Pour in
milk, return to heat but do not boil.
Garnish with chopped chives, parsley
or thyme.

CORN CHOWDER

Stock

1 kg chicken, skin and visible fat
  removed
2 corn cobs, husks removed
1 onion, peeled
1 carrot
2 sprigs fresh parsley
1 × 2-cm piece fresh ginger root,
  peeled

Soup

1 teaspoon fresh ginger root, peeled
  and finely chopped
1 medium onion, peeled and diced
2 teaspoons toasted sesame seeds
6 cups chicken stock (from above)
2 tablespoons dry sherry (optional)
4 tablespoons cornflour
4 tablespoons water
2 egg whites
2 tablespoons water (extra)
6 spring onions, finely chopped

You will use approximately 1 cup of
shredded chicken meat for this soup.
The remaining chicken can be stored
for other meals. The large chicken will
ensure a tasty chicken stock, but you
could substitute chicken carcasses or
chicken breasts.

Place chicken stock ingredients in a
large saucepan and cover with water.
Bring to the boil, reduce heat and
simmer gently for 1½ hours. Remove
chicken and cover immediately with
cold water. This will keep the chicken
meat very moist. Remove from water
when completely cold and refrigerate.

Shred a cup of chicken and set aside.
Strain the stock and discard
ingredients except corn. Reserve
6 cups of stock. Use a sharp knife to
cut through the corn kernels in the
centre from top to bottom. Use the
back edge of the knife to press the
corn flesh out without pulling away
the skin of the kernel. Set aside.

Place chopped ginger, onion and
sesame seeds in a large non-stick
saucepan and cook gently over dry heat
until onions begin to soften
(approximately 2–3 minutes). If onions
begin to stick, add a little stock and
turn down heat. Add chicken stock,
shredded chicken, corn and sherry if
desired and bring to the boil. Mix
cornflour with water to make a paste.
Stir through the soup until it thickens
and then reduce heat. Beat egg whites
lightly with 2 tablespoons water. Add
this to the soup, stirring continuously.
Remove from heat, add spring onions
and serve.

SUMMER CUCUMBER YOGHURT SOUP

Serves 6

2 large cucumbers
2 cups non-fat yoghurt
½ cup low-fat milk or low-fat soy
  milk
2 tablespoons finely chopped chives
  or spring onions
2 teaspoons finely chopped fresh dill
1 Jonathan apple for garnish

Peel cucumbers and cut in half.
Remove seeds and grate flesh.
Combine remaining ingredients and
mix well with grated cucumber. Chill
for several hours so that flavour can
develop. Garnish with thin slices of
apple.

MINESTRONE

Serves 4–6

2 cloves garlic
1 large onion
9 cups vegetable stock or chicken
  stock
2 large carrots, chopped
3 sticks celery and leaves, chopped
1 large potato, chopped
3 small zucchini, chopped
10 green beans, chopped
½ cup sliced mushrooms
2 × 425 g cans tomatoes
black pepper to taste
3 cups cooked haricot beans
½ cup cooked brown rice or ½ cup
  wholemeal macaroni
1 teaspoon dried marjoram

Crush garlic and chop onion. Cook for
6 minutes in ½ cup stock in a large
saucepan. Add remaining stock and
fresh vegetables, then tomatoes.
Season with black pepper. Bring to
the boil and simmer for 1 hour,
stirring occasionally. Purée 2 cups of
soup in a blender and return this to
the soup. Add beans, rice or macaroni
and marjoram and heat through for a
further 5 minutes.

QUICK-AS-A-WINK PUMPKIN SOUP

Serves 6–8

1 medium onion, peeled and chopped

1 teaspoon finely chopped fresh
   ginger root

1 clove garlic, crushed (optional)

800 g pumpkin, peeled and finely
   diced

4 cups defatted chicken stock or
   2 cups unsweetened orange juice
   and 2 cups water

¼ cup salt-free tomato paste

½ teaspoon cumin (optional)

In a large pan cook onion, ginger and
garlic in 2 tablespoons water for
3 minutes or until transparent. To get
the best flavour from onions without
cooking in oil, always place lid on
saucepan while onions are cooking.
Add all other ingredients. Cook for
15–20 minutes or until pumpkin is
tender. Purée. Serve with a thin slice
of orange and garnish with parsley.

SWEET POTATO CURRY AND MINT SOUP

Serves 4–6

1 onion, peeled and diced

500 g sweet potato, peeled and
   chopped

2 teaspoons curry powder (or more
   for a hotter flavour)

4 cups vegetable stock or chicken
   stock

2 teaspoons finely chopped fresh mint

Combine all ingredients, except mint,
and simmer until sweet potato is
tender. Purée and stir through the
mint.

Variation

• For a hearty soup add 1 cup cooked
  brown or red lentils before puréeing.

QUICK AND EASY TOMATO SOUP

Serves 4

1 medium onion, diced
½ teaspoon dried oregano
½ teaspoon dried basil
2 celery sticks, including green
  foliage, diced
2 × 425 g cans salt-free tomatoes
2 tablespoons salt-free tomato paste

Cook onion, herbs and celery in a little water until soft (approximately 3 minutes). Purée tomatoes and tomato paste until smooth. Add to the onion and cook gently for 10–15 minutes. Purée again and serve immediately.

Variations

- Add 1 cup grated raw carrot before serving.
- Add 1 cup finely sliced celery before serving.
- Add 1 cup finely diced mixed red and green capsicum before serving.
- Add ¼ cup finely chopped fresh chives.
- Add 2 teaspoons fresh ginger juice when cooking the onion.
- Add 1 cup potato peeled, diced and cooked before serving.
- Serve chilled tomato soup with non-fat yoghurt and a sprinkling of fresh herbs of your choice.

SALADS AND DRESSINGS

ORANGE, CUCUMBER AND MINT SALAD

Serves 6–8

3 oranges

1 small cucumber

½ cup cider vinegar

2 tablespoons chopped fresh mint

Remove rind and pith from orange and cut into thin rounds. Peel cucumber and cut into thin rounds. Alternate layers of orange and cucumber. Pour over vinegar and sprinkle with mint. Cover and chill. Serve on a bed of lettuce leaves or on alfalfa sprouts.

SWEET RICE

Serves 8

4 cups cooked cold brown rice

½ cup dried apricots, finely chopped

¼ cup currants

¼ cup raisins, finely chopped

¼ cup dried apples, finely chopped

1 medium carrot, diced

2 sticks celery, diced

1 tablespoon sunflower seeds

1 tablespoon sesame seeds, toasted

2 teaspoons grated orange rind

¼ cup unsweetened orange juice

Combine all ingredients and serve immediately.

TABBOULEH RICE

Serves 6
2 cups cooked cold brown rice
4 tomatoes, peeled, seeded and finely
  chopped
4 spring onions, finely chopped
1 cup fresh parsley, finely chopped
1 cup fresh coriander, finely chopped
½ cup fresh mint, finely chopped
¾ cup garlic vinaigrette (see below)

Garlic Vinaigrette
Makes approximately 1¼ cups
¾ cup apple juice
½ cup white wine vinegar
2 tablespoons lemon juice
2 teaspoons grated lemon rind
4 small cloves garlic, peeled and
  halved

To make the vinaigrette, combine all
ingredients in a screw-top jar and keep
in refrigerator. Shake every now and
then. Remove garlic prior to serving,
or remove and crush then return to
vinaigrette.

To make the rice, combine all
ingredients and mix well. Chill. Serve
in a tomato shell, or crisp lettuce cups,
in lettuce leaves rolled up to make a
parcel, or in a cucumber boat.

VEGETABLE RICE SALAD

Serves 6
1 medium carrot, diced
2 small celery sticks, diced
1 small green capsicum, diced
1 small red capsicum, diced
¼ cup corn kernels, cooked
¼ cup peas, cooked
3 cups cooked cold brown rice
2 tablespoons finely chopped fresh
  parsley
2 tablespoons finely chopped fresh
  mint

Combine vegetables in a container of
iced water for 10 minutes. Drain well.
Combine all ingredients and toss well.

For a special treat, remove the tops
from medium-sized tomatoes. Scoop
out flesh, pour rice mixture into
tomatoes and serve.

APPLE SALAD

Serves approximately 6

2 Granny Smith apples

2 Delicious or Jonathan apples

1 small red capsicum

1 small green capsicum

2 sticks celery

2 tablespoons pinenuts, roasted under griller

¼ cup clear apple juice

2 tablespoons lemon juice

1 tablespoon cider vinegar

2 tablespoons finely chopped fresh mint

2 tablespoons finely chopped fresh chives

Core apples and cut into thin wedges. Dice capsicums finely. Cut celery into thin slices. Mix together apples, vegetables and pinenuts. Mix apple juice, lemon juice and vinegar and combine with salad ingredients. Sprinkle with mint and chives. Serve with alfalfa sprouts.

FRUITY COLESLAW

Serves 6–8 as a main course

6 cups finely shredded white cabbage

2 oranges, peeled and segmented

¼ cup dried apricots, cut into thin strips

¼ cup dried peaches, cut into thin strips

¼ cup finely sliced spring onions

¼ cup finely sliced celery

¼ cup shredded coconut (optional)

1 cup fresh pineapple or unsweetened canned pineapple pieces

2 teaspoons grated orange rind

2 teaspoons grated lemon rind

½–1 cup orange dressing

Orange Dressing

1 cup unsweetened orange juice or Viten juice

2 teaspoons arrowroot or cornflour

1–2 teaspoons white wine vinegar

Combine all ingredients in a large salad bowl. Pour over orange dressing and toss well. Leave to stand in refrigerator for at least 1 hour before serving. Serve chilled.

To make the orange dressing, combine all ingredients in a small saucepan. Bring to the boil, stirring until sauce thickens. Cool and refrigerate.

SPICY SPROUTS SALAD

Serves approximately 12
1 cup sultanas
1 cup unsweetened orange juice
½–1 teaspoon cumin
4 celery sticks, finely sliced
150 g mung bean sprouts
150 g lentil sprouts

Soak sultanas in orange juice with cumin for at least 2 hours, or overnight. Combine all ingredients and mix well.

CUCUMBER DRESSING

Makes approximately 1¼ cups
1 cup non-fat yoghurt
½ small cucumber, peeled, seeded and grated
2 tablespoons chopped parsley
2 tablespoons chopped chives
1 tablespoon lemon juice
1 tablespoon vinegar

Combine all ingredients and chill.

CREAMY COTTAGE CHEESE DRESSING

Makes approximately 1 cup
200 g low-fat cottage cheese
1 tablespoon apple juice concentrate
1 tablespoon tarragon vinegar
¼ cup unsweetened apple or pineapple juice

Combine all ingredients in a blender and process until thick and creamy. Refrigerate.

CURRY DRESSING

Makes approximately ½ cup
½ cup non-fat yoghurt
1 teaspoon curry powder
1 teaspoon salt-free tomato paste
1 tablespoon unsweetened orange juice

Mix all ingredients thoroughly and store in refrigerator.

FRENCH DRESSING

Makes approximately 1 cup
2 tablespoons fresh basil or
  1 teaspoon dried basil
½ teaspoon pepper
⅓ cup fresh lemon juice
2 tablespoons fresh parsley
2 teaspoons lemon rind
⅔ cup wine vinegar

Place all ingredients in a sealed jar.
Shake well and store in refrigerator.

ISLAND DRESSING

Makes approximately 1¼ cups
½ cup non-fat yoghurt
½ cup ricotta cheese
juice of 1 lemon
⅓ cup tomato paste
3 drops Tabasco sauce
3 teaspoons chopped green capsicum
finely chopped parsley
finely chopped chives

Put all ingredients except parsley and
chives in blender and process till
smooth. Fold through parsley and
chives and store in refrigerator.

HERB VINAIGRETTE

Makes approximately 1¼ cups
¾ cup unsweetened orange juice
½ cup white wine vinegar
2 tablespoons finely chopped fresh
  oregano
2 tablespoons finely chopped fresh
  chives
2 tablespoons finely chopped fresh
  parsley

Combine all ingredients and mix well.
Store in refrigerator.

MUSTARD DRESSING

Makes approximately 1 cup
1 cup non-fat yoghurt
1 teaspoon dry mustard
1 tablespoon Dijon mustard
1 tablespoon tarragon vinegar

Mix the dry mustard with a small
amount of the yoghurt to blend in
thoroughly. Add this to all other
ingredients. Mix well. Store in
refrigerator.

ORANGE CURRIED SAUCE

Makes 1 cup
1 cup unsweetened orange juice or
   Viten juice
1–2 teaspoons curry powder
2 teaspoons arrowroot

Mix the arrowroot and curry powder
with a small amount of the orange
juice to make a paste. Stir through
remaining orange juice. Place in a
small saucepan. Slowly bring to the
boil until sauce thickens. Cool and
refrigerate.

Use as required. Excellent over
chicken, turkey, cantaloup, cucumbers
and pineapple.

VINAIGRETTE DRESSING

Makes approximately 1¼ cups
¾ cup apple juice
½ cup white wine vinegar
1 teaspoon dry mustard
sprig of fresh rosemary
   (approximately 6 cm)
6 black peppercorns (remove before
   using dressing)
2 teaspoons grated orange rind
1 tablespoon lemon juice
1 tablespoon apple juice concentrate

Combine all ingredients in a screw-top
jar and keep in refrigerator. Shake
every now and then.

MAYONNAISE

Makes 1½ cups
¾ cup low-fat evaporated milk, well
   chilled
¼ cup apple juice concentrate
2 teaspoons Dijon mustard
½ cup wine vinegar

Place ingredients in a screw-top jar
and shake well. Store in refrigerator.
Shake well before each use.

FISH

FISH AND CHIPS

50–90 g (per person) low-fat fish
   fillet
lemon juice
unbleached wholemeal plain flour
egg white
fine wholemeal breadcrumbs
potatoes

Squeeze lemon juice over fish. Dip fish
in flour and shake off excess. Dip in
lightly beaten egg white and press
down in breadcrumbs until both sides
are evenly coated. Shake off excess.
Refrigerate fish in crumbs for at least
2 hours prior to cooking.

Before cooking the fish, prepare the
chips. Preheat oven to 250°C and cut
peeled or unpeeled potatoes into
chips. Place on a non-stick baking
tray. Cook at 250°C for 15 minutes or
until browned.

Add flavour by sprinkling over garlic
powder, onion powder, cayenne pepper
or finely ground skim-milk cheese with
herbs.

Potatoes can be peeled and cut into
chips and quickly sealed in plastic bags
to freeze. Use as required and cook as
above.

Cook the fish in a lightly greased non-
stick pan until both sides are golden
brown (approximately 3 minutes each
side) or place in a lightly floured oven
bag, seal and cook at 200°C for
15–20 minutes.

Fish cooks quickly, so do not
overcook. Fish is cooked when a knife
flakes the flesh easily.

Variation
● To help fish retain moisture and to
   add flavour, fish fillets can be
   marinated in fruit juices with fresh
   herbs, garlic, ginger, tomato paste,
   white wine, non-fat yoghurt and
   spices. Try your own combinations.
   Place fish from marinade into
   breadcrumbs and cook as above.

CHEESY TOPPED FISH DISH

Serves 5

1 clove garlic, finely chopped

½ cup finely chopped spring onions

½ cup finely chopped celery

2 tablespoons finely chopped fresh parsley

5 fillets Blue Grenadier or other suitable fish (approximately 500 g)

1 cup salt-free tomatoes and juice, puréed

½ cup non-fat yoghurt

2 teaspoons low-salt soy sauce

2 teaspoons white wine vinegar

½–1 teaspoon curry powder

½ teaspoon dried tarragon

½ teaspoon dried basil

Topping

1 cup breadcrumbs

½ teaspoon dried basil

1 celery stick, finely chopped

½ cup low-fat grating cheese, grated

Place onion, garlic and celery on the base of an oblong casserole dish. Sprinkle with parsley. Place fish fillets on top of parsley. Mix together tomato purée, yoghurt, soy sauce, vinegar, curry, tarragon and basil. Pour over the fish. Cover and stand for approximately 1 hour. When ready to cook, preheat oven to 180°C.

Mix topping ingredients together. Spread over top of fish. Bake for 35–40 minutes. Serve with a selection of steamed vegetables or brown rice and tossed salad.

TUNA AND VEGETABLE PIE

Serves 6

Crust

6 slices wholemeal bread

Filling

1 medium onion, finely diced

1½ cups low-fat evaporated skim milk or low-fat soy milk

1 tablespoon salt-free tomato paste

1 cup tuna, water-packed, salt-free

1 cup grated carrot

1 cup finely diced celery

1 small green capsicum, finely diced

¼ cup finely chopped fresh parsley

2 tablespoons finely chopped fresh chives

4 tablespoons cornflour

½ cup water

Preheat oven to 200°C.

Crumble the bread into fine breadcrumbs. Lightly grease a small pie dish. Reserve ¾ cup breadcrumbs for topping. Place breadcrumbs in pie dish and spread over base and sides evenly. Firm down with fingers and palm of your hand. Bake at 200°C for 10 minutes. Remove from oven. Turn oven up to 220°C.

While pie crust is cooking, cook onion in 1 tablespoon water in large saucepan for 3 minutes or until transparent. Add milk and simmer 2 minutes. Stir in tomato paste. Add tuna, carrot, celery and capsicum. Simmer, covered, for 5 minutes. Add parsley and chives.

Mix the cornflour with the water to make a thin paste. Stir this through the tuna mixture and cook for 2 minutes, stirring continuously. Cool slightly. Pour into pie crust. Sprinkle with remaining breadcrumbs. Cook at 220°C for 10 minutes. Turn oven down to 200°C and cook for further 20 minutes. Serve with a tossed salad or lightly steamed vegetables.

Opposite
Quick-as-a-Wink Pumpkin Soup
(see page 18) with Herb Scones
(see page 117).

TUNA AND VEGETABLE CASSEROLE

Serves 6

1 × 425 g can tuna
8 spring onions
500 g zucchini, cut into chunks
1 cup thinly sliced broccoli
1 cup thinly sliced cauliflower
1 cup diced carrot
½ cup diced red capsicum plus ½ cup
   diced green capsicum or 1 cup
   frozen peas

Sauce

3 cups low-fat milk or low-fat soy
   milk
½ cup cornflour
1 teaspoon dried oregano
1 teaspoon dried basil
½ cup tomato paste

Topping

½ cup oat bran
½ cup wholemeal or rye breadcrumbs
50 g low-fat grating cheese, grated
½ cup finely chopped fresh parsley

Preheat oven to 180°C.

Drain tuna and add onions. Steam vegetables until just tender and drain. Combine 1 cup milk with cornflour, herbs and tomato paste and mix well. Return this to the remaining milk and heat in a small saucepan until sauce thickens.

Pour sauce over the combined vegetables, onions and tuna in a casserole dish. Combine all topping ingredients and spread evenly over casserole. Bake for 40 minutes or until bubbling and top is golden brown.

This is an excellent casserole to prepare a day ahead; just cover and refrigerate. It will need a little more time in the oven if it goes straight from refrigerator to oven.

Opposite
Tuna and Vegetable Casserole (see this page).

TUNA AND VEGETABLE CROQUETTES

Makes 12 croquettes

1 × 425 g can tuna

1 × 310 g can corn kernels (or 200 g fresh corn kernels)

500 g potatoes, peeled, cooked and mashed

juice of 1 small lemon

100 g carrot, grated

100 g zucchini, grated

100 g onion, finely diced

3 egg whites

1 teaspoon dried dill

1 teaspoon fresh basil (or ¼ teaspoon dried basil)

ground black pepper to taste

1 cup breadcrumbs

Preheat oven to 180°C.

Drain tuna and corn. Combine all ingredients except breadcrumbs and mix well using your hands. Form into small croquettes and roll lightly in breadcrumbs. Refrigerate until firm before cooking.

Lightly grease a non-stick pan and cook croquettes until light brown, a few minutes on each side. Complete cooking by placing on a lined baking tray and cooking for a further 15–20 minutes in the oven.

FISH VEGETABLE BUNDLES

Serves 6

6 fish fillets (approximately 600 g)

julienne strips of carrot, zucchini, green beans, cucumber, red and green capsicums (approximately 8–10 strips per fillet)

1 cup non-fat yoghurt

½ cup non-fat grated cheese

1 cup wholemeal breadcrumbs

2 tablespoons finely chopped fresh parsley

2 tablespoons finely chopped fresh chives

Preheat oven to 180°C.

Roll fish fillets to flatten slightly. Place combination of julienne vegetables in centre of fillet with ends of vegetables visible at either side. Roll up. Place in a shallow, lightly greased ovenproof dish with seam side down. Pour over yoghurt and sprinkle with cheese.

Combine breadcrumbs, parsley and chives. Sprinkle over fish. Cover with foil. Bake for 20–30 minutes or until fish is tender. Remove foil for the last few minutes to brown and crisp breadcrumbs. Serve with salad or steamed vegetables and small steamed potatoes.

SALMON BAKE

Serves 6–8

Base

1 cup cooked brown rice
400 g broccoli, cooked and puréed

Filling

1 medium onion, finely chopped
500 ml low-fat milk or low-fat soy
   milk
¼ cup cornflour
1 × 450 g can salmon, salt-free,
   packed in water
1 teaspoon hot, low-salt mustard
1 medium red capsicum
1 medium green capsicum

Topping

6 slices wholemeal bread
125 g low-fat grating cheese, grated
¼ cup finely chopped fresh parsley

Preheat oven to 190°C.

For the base, combine rice and broccoli and mix well. Spoon onto a shallow lightly greased ovenproof dish.

To make the filling, cook onion for 3 minutes in 2 tablespoons water. Add soy milk, keeping ¼ cup aside. Blend reserved milk with the cornflour to make a paste. Add to heated soy milk, stirring until it thickens. Cook gently for 2 minutes, stirring continuously. Add salmon and mustard and mix well. Remove from heat.

Chop capsicums finely and cook in a small amount of water for 2 minutes to soften. Drain. Add to salmon. Pour over the base.

For topping, make bread into crumbs, add rest of ingredients and mix well. Spoon over top of salmon. Cook in oven for 20–30 minutes until top browns.

CURRY SALMON PATTIES

Makes 4

350 g potatoes, peeled

150 g carrot

220 g red salmon

juice of ½ small lemon

25 g low-fat cheese, grated

½–1 teaspoon curry powder

2 tablespoons finely chopped parsley

2 tablespoons finely chopped spring
onions (green part only)

1 egg white and 2 tablespoons water
(beaten together to combine)

¾ cup wholemeal breadcrumbs and
¼ cup oat bran

Preheat oven to 180°C.

Combine potatoes and carrots, cover with water and cook until just tender. Drain and mash well. Add salmon, lemon juice, cheese, curry, parsley and spring onions and mix well.

Form into patties: two small patties per person, or one large. Dip each patty into combined egg white and water and roll in combined breadcrumbs and oat bran. Lightly grease a non-stick pan and brown patties on both sides for just a few minutes.

Place patties onto a lined baking tray and finish cooking in oven for approximately 15–20 minutes.

MEATS

CABBAGE ROLLS WITH TOMATO SAUCE

Makes 12

1 onion (approximately 100 g), chopped

½ teaspoon fresh ginger root, chopped

½ teaspoon cumin powder

¼ teaspoon coriander powder

2 tablespoons water

600 g lean minced beef (rump, veal)

200 g carrot, grated

100 g zucchini, grated

2 cups cooked brown rice

18 large cabbage leaves (choose green cabbage with thin, soft leaves, and not a hard centre white cabbage, as the leaves break too easily and tend to be stringy)

Tomato Sauce

1 × 425 g can salt-free tomatoes in juice

¼ cup salt-free tomato paste

¼ cup water or dry white wine or vegetable stock

1 large clove garlic

½ teaspoon cumin powder

Cook onion with ginger and spices in water until soft. Add meat and break up. Cover and simmer for 15–20 minutes. Continue to break meat up as it cooks, making sure all meat is well browned and cooked through. Remove from heat. Add all other ingredients and mix well. Cool.

Preheat oven to 200°C.

Place cabbage leaves in boiling water in a large saucepan and cook for 5 minutes to soften. Drain. Do 5 leaves at a time if your pan is not very large. Cut away the hard centre core, but do not cut right through the leaf. Use 1½ leaves to make a whole flat leaf. Use approximately a ½ cup of mixture to make each cabbage roll. Roll up securely, making sure the filling cannot ooze out from the sides.

To make the tomato sauce, purée all ingredients. Pour half the sauce into the bottom of a large, shallow baking dish. Place cabbage rolls, seam side down, on top of sauce and pack tightly together. Pour over remaining sauce. Cover. Bake for 30 minutes. Remove lid and cook a further 15 minutes.

(Alternatively, cabbage rolls can be steamed in a steamer for approximately 30–40 minutes. Tomato sauce can be cooked in a saucepan for 20 minutes or until thickened and poured over steamed cabbage rolls.)

Serve with a boiled or baked potato and an orange vegetable (e.g. pumpkin, carrot) or with a tossed salad. Garnish with fresh parsley.

Variations

- Make other sauces, such as a white sauce (see pages 80–2) with soy milk and ½ cup grated low-fat cheese, to serve over steamed cabbage rolls.
- Sprinkle a cup of wholemeal breadcrumbs over the top of cabbage rolls after 30 minutes cooking time. Cook for a further 15 minutes.
- Sprinkle over ½ cup low-fat grating cheese 10 minutes before cabbage rolls are cooked. Cheese should be just melted, not well browned.

BEEF AND CARROT HOTPOT

Serves 5

500 g lean beef
2 cloves garlic, crushed
1 large onion, peeled and chopped
1 cup dry red wine
½–1 teaspoon nutmeg
2 cups beef stock or water
2 tablespoons salt-free tomato paste
500 g carrot, cut into chunks
3 bay leaves
2 tablespoons finely chopped fresh parsley

Preheat oven to 190°C.

Cut meat into small pieces and then stir-fry in a large frying pan (in 2 lots) to seal and lightly brown. Remove from pan. Stir-fry onions and garlic until onions are transparent (approximately 2–3 minutes). Return meat to pan. Add red wine and nutmeg and cook for 5 minutes. Add tomato paste and stock. Pour into a casserole dish. Add carrots and bay leaves. Toss well, cover and bake for 1¼ hours or until meat is tender. Add parsley before serving.

Serve with hot mashed potato, brown rice or wholemeal noodles.

FRUITY BEEF LUNCHEON LOAF

Serves 10–12

5 cups wholemeal breadcrumbs (for topping)

150 g lean minced beef

1 medium onion, finely diced

400 g potato, grated

400 g carrot, grated

125 g dried apricots, finely chopped

125 g sultanas

125 g raisins

2 cups wholemeal breadcrumbs

⅓ cup salt-free tomato paste or mango chutney (see page 49)

1 tablespoon low-salt soy sauce

½–1 teaspoon cumin powder

½ teaspoon coriander powder

½ teaspoon mixed spice

Preheat oven to 220°C.

Line a dish measuring approximately 40 cm × 30 cm × 6 cm with lightly greased foil. Press 2 cups breadcrumbs firmly onto base of dish. Combine all ingredients except remaining 3 cups of topping breadcrumbs and mix well with hands. Press into dish on top of breadcrumb base and firm down. Top with breadcrumbs and firm down again.

Cook at 220°C for 20 minutes. Turn heat down to 190°C and cook for further 50–55 minutes. Remove from oven. Excellent served hot or cold with a salad. If serving hot, let stand for 10 minutes before slicing.

BEEF 'STROGANOFF'

Serves 6

500 g lean rump steak

2 medium onions, peeled and chopped

250 g carrot, cut into thin rounds
and then quartered

600 g mushrooms, thinly sliced

1 tablespoon Vecon (a natural
vegetable concentrate available at
health food shops)

1 cup boiling water

1 cup dry red wine

2 tablespoons salt-free tomato paste

ground black pepper

1 cup low-fat milk or low-fat soy
milk

1 tablespoon and 1 teaspoon
cornflour

Preheat oven to 200°C.

Cut steak into bite-sized pieces. In a large pan stir-fry meat to seal and lightly brown. Remove meat from the pan. Stir-fry onions until transparent (approximately 2–3 minutes). Add carrots and mushrooms and toss to combine. Dissolve Vecon in boiling water and add to pan. Simmer for 3 minutes. Return meat to pan. Add red wine and tomato paste and season to taste with black pepper.

Transfer to an ovenproof casserole dish and cook, covered, in oven for 1¼ hours. Combine soy milk and cornflour. Remove casserole from heat and allow to cool slightly. Stir through the soy milk and cornflour until sauce becomes thick and creamy. Serve with mashed or baked potatoes.

ZUCCHINI MEATLOAF

Serves 10–12

400 g zucchini, grated
500 g lean minced beef (rump)
1 medium onion, finely chopped
100 g red capsicum, finely chopped
2 cups wholemeal breadcrumbs
1 egg white
2 tablespoons salt-free tomato paste
1 tablespoon finely chopped fresh
    tarragon or parsley
1 tablespoon finely chopped fresh
    basil
ground black pepper to taste
¼ cup low-fat grating cheese, grated

Preheat oven to 180°C.

Combine all ingredients except cheese. Using hands mix all ingredients thoroughly. Press mixture into a foil-lined terrine dish. Press down firmly and cover with foil. Place terrine in a large pan of water so that the water reaches at least 2 cm up the side of the terrine dish. Cook at 180°C for 1¼ hours.

Drain off any liquid and unmould terrine onto a foil-lined baking tray. Sprinkle over cheese. Return to oven to cook a further 10 minutes. Let stand 10 minutes before slicing if serving hot, or cool and refrigerate.

Serve as a meat luncheon loaf with salads or use in sandwiches or on wholemeal biscuits.

SPAGHETTI AND MEATBALLS

Serves 6
600 g wholemeal spaghetti

Meatballs
250 g lean beef or veal, finely minced
1 onion, finely minced
1 cup wholemeal breadcrumbs
1 Granny Smith apple, peeled and
    grated

Tomato Sauce
1 onion, peeled and diced
1 small green capsicum, chopped
1 small red capsicum, chopped
1 × 425 g can salt-free tomatoes
1 cup water
2 tablespoons salt-free tomato paste
½ teaspoon dried basil
½ teaspoon dried oregano
¼ cup fresh parsley, finely chopped

Combine all meatball ingredients and roll into very small balls. Place in a shallow pan in approximately 3 cm water. Bring to the boil, turn heat down and simmer, covered, for about 8 minutes. Remove from pan and drain.

To make the tomato sauce, cook onion and capsicum in a little water to soften (approximately 3 minutes). Purée tomatoes and add them with the water. Bring to the boil. Add tomato paste, basil and oregano. Cook for 20 minutes. Sauce should boil and thicken and slightly reduce. Add meatballs to sauce and heat through.

Boil 2 litres of water while making sauce. Add wholemeal spaghetti and cook until tender. Serve sauce and meatballs over spaghetti and sprinkle with fresh parsley.

BEEF BURGER WITH THE LOT

Makes approximately 10 burgers

500 g lean minced beef (rump, porterhouse or fillet)

200 g carrot, grated

200 g zucchini, grated

200 g Granny Smith apples, peeled and grated

400 g potato, peeled and grated

1 cup wholemeal breadcrumbs, firmly packed

2 tablespoons wholemeal plain flour

¼ cup finely chopped fresh parsley

½ teaspoon nutmeg

½ teaspoon dried mixed herbs

Combine all ingredients and mix with hands. Shape into equal-sized balls. Flatten. Place in a lightly greased pan and cook on moderate heat for approximately 6 minutes. Carefully turn over and cook for a further 4–5 minutes. Remove from pan and rest on absorbent paper for a few minutes.

Serve in a wholemeal burger bun or between 2 wholemeal pita breads. Add shredded lettuce, onion rings, tomato slices, grated carrot, red and green capsicum rings, bean sprouts. Top with some home-made tomato chutney.

BEEF AND CAPSICUM

Serves 6

500 g lean beef (an eye fillet would be an excellent choice)

1 large onion, peeled and cut into 8 pieces

1 green capsicum, cut into chunks

1 red capsicum, cut into chunks

2 sticks celery, sliced diagonally

Sauce

1 teaspoon finely chopped fresh ginger root

1 tablespoon salt-free tomato paste

1 tablespoon low-salt soy sauce

½ teaspoon dried basil

½ teaspoon dried oregano

2 cups beef stock or water

2 tablespoons cornflour

Slice meat into strips. Stir-fry (in 3 lots) to seal meat and lightly brown. Remove meat from pan. Add onion, capsicum and celery and toss, cooking for 2 minutes. Return meat to pan.

Pour over combined sauce ingredients. Bring to the boil and then reduce heat. Simmer with lid on for 20–30 minutes. Stir occasionally so meat does not stick to base of pan. Serve with hot mashed potato or brown rice.

SPICY LAMB AND RICE

Serves 10–12

2 cups uncooked brown rice
1 kg lean lamb
2 medium onions, finely diced
½–1 teaspoon coriander powder
½ teaspoon ginger powder
½–1 teaspoon cumin powder
1 cup beef or vegetable stock
2 green capsicums, cut into small
  pieces
2 carrots, cut into small pieces
2 cups sultanas
2 celery sticks, cut into small pieces

Cook rice in boiling water until tender, drain and set aside. Mince lamb and remove sinew.

In a large saucepan cook onion for 3 minutes or until soft in a small amount of water. Add meat and spices. Simmer, covered, for 30 minutes.

Break meat up into small pieces as it cooks so it retains its minced texture. Add stock as necessary so meat does not dry out; but as this is a dry dish, avoid adding too much liquid. Add vegetables and sultanas and cook, covered, for 10 minutes. Fold through the cooked, drained rice. Serve in crisp lettuce cups or in half-baked eggplant shells.

BEEF AND BEANS

Serves 6

400 g fat-free minced beef (rump,
    porterhouse or fillet)
1 large onion, peeled and chopped
2 cloves garlic, crushed
2 sticks celery, finely chopped
2 small green capsicums, chopped
400 g green beans
2 tablespoons low-salt soy sauce
1 tablespoon toasted sesame seeds
1 cup salt-free tomatoes and juice,
    puréed
½ cup of water

Cook meat, onion and garlic in a large
saucepan in a small amount of water,
stirring occasionally to break up meat,
for 10–15 minutes. Keep covered. Add
remaining ingredients and simmer,
with lid off, for 15 minutes. Serve on
wholemeal toast, brown rice or
wholemeal pasta, or cooked beans and
lentils.

LAMB ROAST DINNER WITH VEGETABLES

1–2 kg boned piece of lean shoulder
    lamb
unbleached wholemeal flour
ground black pepper

Stuffing

1¾ cups wholemeal breadcrumbs
10 dried apricots, finely chopped
1 apple, peeled and grated
¼ cup finely chopped fresh parsley
½ teaspoon dried sage

Gravy

2 tablespoons low-salt tomato paste
arrowroot

Preheat oven to 220°C.

Combine all stuffing ingredients, mix
well and fill cavity in meat. Secure
ends with fine meat skewers. Roll
meat in wholemeal flour, seasoned
with ground black pepper, and shake
off excess. Place in an oven bag. Cook
at 220°C for 25 minutes per half-kilo
of lamb weight.

When cooked, pour off excess juice
and remove fat. Add tomato paste and
water. Allow ¼ cup water per person.
Simmer and thicken with arrowroot

(combine arrowroot with water to make a paste).

Serve with any of the following vegetables: potatoes, pumpkin, peas, Brussels sprouts, cauliflower, carrots, beans, spinach, parsnip, corn, zucchini, cabbage, sweet potatoes, yellow squash, broccoli, tomatoes or red and green capsicums.

Vegetables can be steamed or baked. To bake vegetables, place on a non-stick baking tray or place in an oven bag. Follow cooking instructions on oven-bag packet.

LAMB CURRY

Serves 10
1 kg boned lean lamb
1 large onion, peeled and chopped
1 teaspoon finely chopped fresh
　ginger root
1 cup chopped carrot
1 cup chopped beans
1 cup chopped celery
1 cup chopped green capsicum
1 cup sultanas

Sauce
3 cups lamb stock or water
3 tablespoons salt-free tomato paste
3 tablespoons cornflour
2 teaspoons curry powder
½ teaspoon cumin powder
rind of ½ lemon, cut into thin strips

Preheat oven to 190°C.

Mince lamb, removing any sinew. In a large wok, or very large saucepan, stir-fry lamb (in 3 lots) to seal meat and lightly brown. Remove from pan and set aside. Stir-fry onion and ginger until onion is transparent (approximately 2–3 minutes). Add vegetables and sultanas, tossing to combine. Add meat and combined sauce ingredients. Place in a casserole dish. Cook in oven for 1 hour.

MEXICAN LAMB BALLS WITH SWEET POTATOES AND PEAS

Serves 6

400 g lean lamb
1 medium onion, finely diced
2 cups wholemeal breadcrumbs
1¾ cups water
12 medium sweet potatoes
3 cups peas

Sauce

1 medium onion, diced
2 cloves garlic, crushed (optional)
½ teaspoon finely chopped fresh
  ginger root
1 cup stock (liquid in which
  meatballs are cooked)
1 × 400 g can salt-free tomatoes in
  juice, puréed
¼ cup salt-free tomato paste
2 tablespoons low-salt soy sauce
1 large red capsicum
4 spring onions
2 sticks celery

Mince lamb and mix with onion and breadcrumbs. Roll mixture into small balls (approximately 20). Place in a shallow pan. Cover with water and bring to the boil. Place lid on and turn heat down to simmer. Cook for approximately 30 minutes. Remove meatballs and retain stock.

Preheat oven to 210°C.

Place onion, garlic and ginger in a saucepan. Add a little stock. Place lid on and cook for 3 minutes. Add tomatoes, tomato paste, rest of stock and soy sauce. Cook for 10 minutes. Cut capsicum in half. Remove seeds and cut into long strips. Cut onions and celery into small diagonal pieces.

Place meatballs in a casserole dish and add capsicum, onion and celery. Pour over sauce. Place lid on casserole. Bake in oven for 30 minutes. Serve with 2 medium-sized sweet potatoes and ½ cup green peas per person.

To cook sweet potatoes, peel and cut into cubes. Simmer until just tender.

CHICKEN BURGERS

Makes 4

200 g chicken, with fat and skin removed

1 Granny Smith apple, peeled and grated

50 g low-fat grating cheese

1 cup wholemeal breadcrumbs

2 tablespoons finely chopped fresh chives

2 tablespoons finely chopped fresh parsley

Mango Chutney

1 onion, peeled and diced

1 teaspoon finely chopped fresh ginger root

¼ cups water or chicken stock

flesh of 2 mangoes (approximately 420 g)

2 Granny Smith apples, peeled and grated

1 cup unsweetened orange juice

⅓ cup brown rice vinegar (macrobiotic, available at health food stores)

½ teaspoon chilli powder

½ teaspoon cumin powder

rind of 1 orange

½ cup apple juice concentrate

Mince chicken. Add other burger ingredients and mix well. Form into 4 balls and flatten. Cook in a non-stick pan for 2 minutes on both sides. Serve in a wholemeal burger bun or between 2 wholemeal pita breads. Add shredded lettuce, cucumber slices, grated carrot, alfalfa sprouts, thin slices of apple, bean shoots or sliced celery. Top with some home-made mango chutney.

To make the chutney, simmer onion and ginger in chicken stock for 5 minutes. Add all other ingredients. Cover and bring to the boil. Remove lid and cook for 1 hour. Stir frequently to prevent chutney sticking to base of saucepan. Cool. Pour into sterilised jars. Keep refrigerated.

Variations

- If doubling recipe, do not double quantity of cheese. Add 25 g extra cheese for 200 g extra chicken.
- When mangoes are out of season you can substitute canned unsweetened peaches. Drain before using.

BRAISED CHINESE VEGETABLES WITH CHICKEN

Serves 4

400 g chicken, with fat and skin
   removed
30 g Chinese dried mushrooms
1 × 250 g can bamboo shoot (rinse
   off excess salt under water)
1 teaspoon crushed ginger
¼ cup chicken stock
1 tablespoon dry sherry
2 teaspoons apple juice concentrate
200 g broccoli, thinly sliced
100 g celery, diagonally sliced
2 tablespoons chicken stock, extra
1 teaspoon cornflour

Chop chicken into bite-sized pieces.
Cover the dried mushrooms with hot
water and stand for 15 minutes or
until mushrooms are softened. Drain
and slice the mushrooms thinly. Slice
bamboo shoot.

Place chicken, mushrooms, bamboo
shoot, ginger, stock, sherry and apple
juice concentrate in a wok. Simmer
with lid on until chicken is just
tender. Add celery and broccoli,
cover and simmer until vegetables are
just tender. Combine extra stock and
cornflour. Add to the wok and bring
to the boil. Stir continuously and
cook for 1 minute. Serve
immediately.

CHICKEN SWEET AND SOUR

Serves 6

500 g chicken, with fat and skin
  removed
1 medium red capsicum
1 medium green capsicum
2 medium carrots
2 medium zucchini
6 spring onions
3 sticks celery
½ cup chopped pineapple

Sauce

1 cup unsweetened apple juice
1 teaspoon finely chopped fresh
  ginger
2 teaspoons low-salt soy sauce
1 tablespoon salt-free tomato paste
1 clove garlic, crushed (optional)

Cut chicken into 2-cm chunks. Cut vegetables into even-sized pieces.

Combine all sauce ingredients in a wok or large, shallow pan. Bring to the boil and simmer gently. Add chicken. Cook for 15–20 minutes or until tender.

Remove chicken. Turn up heat. Add all vegetables and cook for 2 minutes, tossing continuously through the sauce. Add chicken and pineapple. Place lid on wok or pan and cook a further minute.

CHICKEN CASSEROLE WITH SNOW PEAS

Serves 4

400 g chicken meat, with skin and
    fat removed
½ teaspoon cumin
½ teaspoon coriander powder
2 cups chicken stock
200 g carrot
200 g zucchini
100 g celery
2 tablespoons cornflour
2 tablespoons water
100 g snow peas
5 spring onions

Cut the chicken into bite-sized pieces.
Heat a large non-stick pan to
moderately hot and add chicken
pieces. Keep tossing to seal the meat.
This will take approximately 3
minutes. Add spices and continue to
toss. Add stock and bring to the boil.
Reduce heat to simmer and cook for
10–15 minutes.

Cut carrots and zucchini into rounds
and then quarters. Slice the celery
diagonally. Add to meat, cover and
simmer for a further 10 minutes. Add
combined cornflour and water. Top
and tail snow peas, slice onions
diagonally and add to pan. Cook
5–8 minutes, stirring continuously.
Serve on a bed of wholemeal
spaghetti.

CHICKEN CHAUSSEUR

Serves 6–8

1 kg chicken drumsticks and wings,
  with skin and fat removed
400 g mushrooms
2 cloves garlic, crushed
2 tablespoons low-salt soy sauce
1 cup dry white wine
1 × 425 g can salt-free tomatoes,
  puréed
2 tablespoons salt-free tomato paste
¼ teaspoon dried tarragon
600 g carrot, cut into chunks
¼ cup chopped spring onions
2 tablespoons finely chopped fresh
  parsley

Sauce

1 onion, thinly sliced
½ cup grated parsnip
⅓ cup cornflour
3 cups chicken stock

Preheat oven to 200°C.

Stir-fry chicken to seal meat and slightly brown. Do in 3 lots. Remove chicken and set aside.

Stir-fry onion and parsnip for the sauce until onion is transparent (approximately 3 minutes). Add combined cornflour and stock. Bring to the boil, reduce heat and simmer for 10 minutes. Remove sauce from pan and set aside.

Wash pan and stir-fry garlic and mushrooms in soy sauce until mushrooms are soft. Add wine and boil until liquid has reduced by half. Add combined puréed tomatoes, tomato paste and tarragon. Stir to combine.

Add onion and parsnip sauce to the pan. Add chicken and carrots. Cover or place in a covered casserole dish. Bake in oven for 40 minutes or until chicken and carrots are tender. If cooking on top of the stove, keep casserole simmering, stirring occasionally so ingredients do not stick to the base of pan.

When the casserole is cooked top with spring onions and parsley, and serve with brown rice, mashed potato or wholemeal noodles.

CHICKEN AND FRUIT CURRY

Serves 4–6

400 g chicken meat, with skin and
    fat removed

2 cloves garlic, crushed

1 large onion, diced

1 tablespoon curry powder

2 cups chicken stock

2 bay leaves

1 × 425 g can unsweetened apricot
    halves, drained

1 × 440 g can unsweetened
    pineapple pieces, drained

6 water chestnuts, thinly sliced

1 cup low-fat milk or low-fat soy
    milk

1 tablespoon and 1 teaspoon
    cornflour

Cut chicken into 2-cm chunks. Stir-fry chicken on a hot, non-stick surface to seal meat and lightly brown (approximately 3 minutes). Remove chicken from pan. Add garlic, onion and curry powder. Toss continuously until onion is transparent (approximately 2–3 minutes).

Add chicken stock and bay leaves and bring to the boil. Add chicken meat and simmer for 20 minutes or until chicken is tender. Add apricots, pineapple and water chestnuts. Combine soy milk and cornflour to make a paste. Add, stirring continuously until sauce boils and thickens. Serve with brown rice.

MANGO CURRY CHICKEN SALAD

Serves 4

1 mango (yielding approximately
   ½ cup mango juice)
1 cup non-fat or low-fat yoghurt
½ teaspoon curry powder
½ teaspoon cumin powder
400 g cooked chicken (no skin or
   fat), broken into pieces

Peel mango and remove flesh from
stone. Push through a sieve. Add
yoghurt and spices and mix well. Add
chicken pieces and coat well.
Refrigerate for at least 2 hours before
serving.

Serve chicken salad on a bed of
lettuce, sprinkled with chopped chives
and garnished with fresh mango slices
or fresh peach slices, slices of kiwi
fruit and alfalfa sprouts.

VEGETARIAN DISHES

MEXICAN BEAN TORTILLAS

Serves 2

2 tortillas
1 cup Quick and Easy Tomato Sauce
2 cups cooked red kidney beans
shredded lettuce
1 tomato, seeded and chopped
¼ cup chopped spring onions
¼ cup cooked corn kernels
2 radishes, thinly sliced
2 tablespoons non-fat or low-fat
   yoghurt

Quick and Easy Tomato Sauce

1 onion, peeled and finely diced
1 teaspoon crushed garlic
1 × 425 g can tomatoes, roughly
   chopped or 500 g fresh tomatoes,
   peeled, seeded and chopped
½ cup tomato paste
½ teaspoon dried basil
½ teaspoon dried oregano
black pepper to taste

To make the tomato sauce, sauté onion and garlic in a medium saucepan over low heat until onion begins to soften. Add all other ingredients. Simmer, uncovered, for 10 minutes.

Heat tortillas in a hot oven until crisp. In a pan heat 1 cup tomato sauce (add a little Tabasco sauce for a hotter taste if desired). Take one cup of the kidney beans and mash them. Add mashed beans to tomato sauce. Spread this equally over tortillas. Combine all salad ingredients and add to tortillas. Top with remaining beans, and a tablespoon of yoghurt per tortilla. Serve immediately.

MINESTRONE STEW

Serves 8–10

100 g haricot or red kidney beans

2 cloves garlic, crushed

1 medium leek, chopped

2 cups vegetable or chicken stock or
water

100 g carrot, chopped

100 g celery, chopped

100 g zucchini, chopped

100 g potato, peeled and chopped

10 green beans, topped and tailed

10 medium mushrooms, cut in half

2 × 425g cans salt-free tomatoes

1 teaspoon dried basil

1 teaspoon dried marjoram

3 tablespoons cornflour

¼ cup water

¼ cup finely chopped fresh parsley

2 tablespoons finely chopped fresh
chives

Soak beans overnight. Drain and
cover with water. Bring to the boil,
reduce heat and simmer for 1–1½
hours or until beans are tender. Drain.

Place garlic, leek and stock in a
medium-sized casserole or saucepan.
Simmer for 10 minutes. Cut green
beans into 4, and add to pan with
remaining ingredients except the
haricot beans, cornflour, water, parsley
and chives. Cook until vegetables are
tender.

Mix cornflour with water. Add to the
casserole. Bring to the boil and stir to
thicken. Reduce heat. Add haricot
beans and herbs. Serve with
wholemeal noodles or wholemeal
toast.

CHILLI BEAN SALAD ON WHOLEMEAL PITA BREADS

Serves 6

6 small wholemeal pita breads
shredded lettuce
6–8 medium tomatoes
1 quantity chilli beans, warm or cold
   (see pages 79–80)

Top pita breads with shredded lettuce.
Cut tomatoes into quarters, remove
seeds and cut each quarter into 4 thin
strips. Make a circle of strips around
the outside edge of pita breads. Top
with chilli bean mixture. Garnish, if
desired, with thin strips of carrot and
alfalfa sprouts.

VEGETARIAN 'CHILLI CON CARNE'

Serves 10–12

2 cups red kidney beans
12 large potatoes
2 small onions, chopped
2 cloves garlic, crushed
300 g carrot, chopped
400 g green beans, sliced
2 small red capsicums, chopped
1 × 300 ml can salt-free tomato juice
2 × 425 g cans salt-free tomatoes
   and juice
1–2 teaspoons chilli powder
½ cup finely chopped fresh parsley

Cover beans with water and soak
overnight. Drain. Cover with clean
cold water. Bring to the boil, reduce
heat and simmer for 1 hour or until
beans are tender. Drain and reserve
cooking liquid.

While the beans are cooking, heat
oven to 180°C, prick the potatoes all
over and bake them.

Towards the end of the potatoes'
cooking time, heat onion and garlic in
a little water in a large, covered pan
until soft and transparent
(approximately 3 minutes). Add
vegetables and ½ cup of cooking liquid

from the beans. Simmer uncovered until vegetables begin to soften. Add tomato juice, tomatoes and chilli powder. Cook gently for 20 minutes. Add beans. Sprinkle over parsley and serve in a scooped-out baked potato. Mash extra potato and pipe on top. Reheat in oven if necessary.

CAULIFLOWER CHEESE BAKE

Serves 4

300 g carrot, cut into rounds
500 g cauliflower florets
2 cups low-fat milk or low-fat soy
 milk
2 bay leaves
black pepper to taste
2 tablespoons finely chopped fresh
 parsley
4 tablespoons cornflour
100 g low-fat grating cheese, finely
 grated

Preheat oven to 200°C.

Steam carrots and cauliflower until just tender. Combine remaining ingredients except cornflour and cheese in a small saucepan. Mix cornflour with a small amount of water to make a paste. Bring the soy milk and herbs to just below boiling. Stir through the cornflour briskly to make a thick sauce. Remove bay leaves.

Place carrots on the base of a shallow casserole dish. Top with cauliflower and pour over the white sauce. Sprinkle with cheese. Bake for 10–15 minutes or until top is browned.

CARROT AND BROCCOLI QUICHE

Serves 6

Base

3 cups wholemeal breadcrumbs
2 tablespoons tomato paste

Filling

200 g broccoli florets
200 g carrot, cut into chunks
1 cup evaporated skim milk
200 g cottage cheese
200 g egg whites
1 cup fresh herbs (e.g. mixed chives,
    parsley, basil), finely chopped

Preheat oven to 180°C.

Combine breadcrumbs and tomato paste in food processor until the mixture just begins to stick together. Press into a lightly oiled quiche dish, making sure sides are even and come up to the top of the dish. Firm base and edges, otherwise quiche will be crumbly. Bake for 10 minutes. Set aside to cool.

Steam broccoli florets and carrot chunks until just tender. Drain well. Place milk, cheese, egg whites and herbs in food processor. Blend until well mixed and cheese is smooth. Place vegetables over cooked base and pour over the cheese mixture. Bake in oven until centre is firm (approximately 30–40 minutes).

CARROT TERRINE

Serves 10–12

500 g carrot, peeled and chopped

250 g potato, peeled and chopped

1 large onion, finely chopped

2 bay leaves

½ cup salt-free and sugar-free tomato juice

¼ cup vegetable or chicken stock

½ cup unbleached wholemeal plain flour

½ teaspoon dried sage

2 teaspoons dried basil

1 teaspoon dried oregano

4 egg whites

Preheat oven to 190°C.

Simmer the first six ingredients in a covered saucepan for 20 minutes or until vegetables are soft. Remove bay leaves and purée vegetables. Add flour and herbs and mix well.

Beat egg whites until light and fluffy. Fold through the mixture. Pour into a lightly greased glass terrine dish (approximately 20 cm × 10 cm). Cover with foil. Bake for 40–60 minutes. Terrine is cooked when a knife inserted into the centre comes out clean. Rest for 5–10 minutes before serving. The terrine is best eaten cold so refrigerate after terrine is cooled.

Serve in wholegrain rolls, salt-free, oil-free rye crispbread or with salad or vegetable crudités.

Variation

- Spread 1½ cups whipped low-fat ricotta cheese on top of the terrine. Decorate with parsley or cucumber.

CHINESE CORN AND VEGETABLE COMBINATION

Serves 4–6

2 teaspoons finely chopped fresh
  ginger root
2 cloves garlic, crushed
1 tablespoon low-salt soy sauce
2 tablespoons Chinese wine or dry
  sherry
½ cup unsweetened orange juice
2 medium onions, quartered
3 sticks celery, sliced diagonally
250 g green beans, sliced diagonally
250 g carrot, sliced diagonally
125 g mushrooms, sliced
125 g snow peas, stringed, topped
  and tailed
1 × 225 g can baby corn, rinsed
1 cup Chinese Chicken Stock (see
  below)
1 tablespoon cornflour
200 g fresh bean shoots

Chinese Chicken Stock

1 kg chicken or chicken pieces or
  chicken carcasses
2 litres water
3-cm piece fresh ginger root, peeled
  and sliced
4 peppercorns
1 onion, peeled and sliced
3 sprigs of parsley

Add the first 5 ingredients to a cold
wok. Slowly bring to the boil and
simmer for 2 minutes.

Add onion and celery. Toss to
combine ingredients and cook,
covered, for 2 minutes.

Add beans, carrot, mushrooms and
snow peas. Toss and cook for
3 minutes.

Add corn and cook, covered, for
1 minute.

To make the Chinese chicken stock,
place all ingredients in a large
saucepan and bring to the boil.
Simmer for 1½ hours. Cool, remove
scum, strain and use liquid only.

Pour over combined stock and
cornflour. Return to the boil. Add
bean shoots. Cook, covered, for
1 minute. Serve immediately.

MUSHROOM MINI PIES

Makes 6

6 small foil pie plates
6 slices wholemeal bread
100 g mushrooms, finely chopped
150 g zucchini, finely grated
100 g fresh tomato, peeled and finely chopped
2 tablespoons finely chopped fresh parsley
1 teaspoon dried oregano
1 teaspoon dried basil
3 egg whites
½ cup non-fat yoghurt
100 g low-fat grating cheese, grated

Preheat oven to 220°C.

Lightly grease foil pie plates. Roll bread out flat using a rolling pin. Use scissors to cut out a round to fit pie plate. Press into pie plates and trim edges with scissors.

Combine mushrooms, zucchini, tomato, parsley and herbs.

Beat egg whites and add yoghurt. Fold in cheese and add to vegetables. Spoon into cases. Use the bread scraps to make breadcrumbs. Sprinkle breadcrumbs over pies.

Cook at 220°C for 15 minutes and then turn oven down to 200°C and cook for a further 15 minutes. Serve hot or cold.

MACARONI WITH VEGETABLES AND CHEESE TOPPING

Serves 6–8

200 g wholemeal macaroni or
    soyaroni noodles
225 g carrot, diced
225 g zucchini, diced
4 sticks celery, chopped
2 cups vegetable stock or water
2 cups low-fat milk or low-fat soy milk
¾ cup cornflour
½ cup fresh parsley, finely chopped
1 cup low-fat grating cheese, grated

Preheat oven to 200°C.

Cook macaroni in boiling water until
tender. Drain. Cook vegetables in
stock until tender. Drain and keep
liquid. Cool stock slightly. Add 1½
cups milk and bring to almost boiling.
Combine ½ cup milk with cornflour
and stir to make a paste. Stir through
remaining milk and vegetable stock,
stirring continuously until stock
thickens.

Add parsley and cheese. Combine
vegetables and macaroni in an
ovenproof dish. Pour over cheese
sauce. Cook at 200°C for 15–20
minutes or until top begins to brown.

SPAGHETTI WITH TOMATO AND VEGETABLE SAUCE

Serves 6

600 g wholemeal spaghetti

Sauce

1 large onion, peeled and diced
1 medium green capsicum
1 medium red capsicum
2 sticks celery, finely chopped
1 cup finely chopped green beans
1 cup finely chopped carrot
1 × 425 g can salt-free tomatoes and
    juice, puréed
¼ cup salt-free tomato paste
1 cup water
½ teaspoon dried basil
½ teaspoon dried oregano
2 bay leaves

Cook onion in a very lightly oiled
saucepan, stirring, until just
transparent (approximately 2–3
minutes). Finely chop capsicums and
add to pan. Add remaining sauce
ingredients. Bring to the boil. Reduce
heat and simmer for 30–40 minutes.

Boil 2 litres of water while making sauce. Add wholemeal spaghetti and cook until tender.

Serve sauce over cooked spaghetti. Sprinkle with finely chopped parsley or low-fat grating cheese, or a combination of both.

MUSHROOM QUICHE

Serves 6

Base
3 cups wholemeal breadcrumbs
2 tablespoons tomato paste

Filling
20 medium mushrooms
1 cup evaporated skim milk
250 g cottage cheese
200 g egg whites
lots of black pepper to taste
1 cup chopped spring onions

Preheat oven to 180°C.

Combine breadcrumbs and tomato paste in food processor until the mixture just begins to stick together. Press into a lightly oiled quiche dish. Cook for 10 minutes. Remove from oven and cool.

Steam mushrooms until soft. Drain and add juice to milk. Combine milk, cottage cheese and egg whites in food processor and blend until smooth. Add black pepper to taste and fold in the spring onions.

Pour mixture over the cooked base and place mushrooms evenly in mixture with tops up. Bake until centre is firm, about 30–40 minutes.

MUSHROOM CAPS

Serves 6–12

12 large mushrooms, stems removed

2 tablespoons mashed potato for each
  mushroom

1 tablespoon grated low-fat grating
  cheese for each mushroom

2 tablespoons finely ground
  wholemeal breadcrumbs for each
  mushroom

Preheat oven to 220°C.

Place mushrooms top down on a
lightly greased non-stick baking tray.
Fill each mushroom with potato. Top
with cheese. Sprinkle over
breadcrumbs and firm down. Bake for
8–10 minutes. Serve with salad.

MUSHROOM AND POTATO PIE

Serves 4–6

900 g potato, peeled and cubed

4 sticks celery, finely chopped

1 medium onion, peeled and finely
  diced

2 cloves garlic, crushed

1 medium carrot, grated

400 g mushrooms, thinly sliced

2 tablespoons cornflour

200 ml low-fat milk or low-fat soy
  milk

2 tablespoons finely chopped fresh
  parsley

1 teaspoon dried thyme

2 teaspoons lemon juice

pinch of cayenne pepper

Preheat oven to 190°C.

Cook potatoes in boiling water until
tender. Drain and mash until smooth.
Add a little milk if necessary.

Place celery, onion and garlic in a
saucepan and cook until soft and
transparent. Add 2 tablespoons water
to avoid sticking to base of saucepan if
necessary. Add carrot and mushrooms
and cook for further 10 minutes.

Blend cornflour and milk and stir into the mushrooms. Add parsley, thyme, lemon juice and cayenne pepper. Simmer for 5 minutes. Pour mixture into a lightly greased ovenproof dish. Spoon mashed potatoes over and spread evenly. Cook for 20 minutes or until potato begins to brown.

POTATO WHIP WITH VEGETABLES

Serves 6–8

4 cups potato, peeled
1 cup green peas
1 cup diced carrot
½ cup diced green capsicum
½ cup diced red capsicum
low-fat milk or low-fat soy milk
½ cup finely grated low-fat grating cheese
1–2 tablespoons finely chopped fresh parsley

Steam or boil the vegetables separately until cooked. Drain and keep hot.

Mash potatoes with a little milk to bind. Combine with other ingredients in a piping bag. Pipe onto a plate and serve with wholemeal toast fingers.

POTATO HUNZA PIE

Makes 8–10 slices

1.25 kg potato, peeled and cubed
1 small bunch spinach, cleaned and
    roughly chopped
1 cup chopped spring onions
1 teaspoon nutmeg
pinch of cayenne pepper
6 sheets filo pastry
2 tablespoons sesame seeds or poppy
    seeds (optional)

Preheat oven to 220°C.

Steam potatoes until tender and drain.
Steam spinach until cooked and drain.
Combine potatoes, spinach, spring
onions, nutmeg and cayenne pepper.
Mix well.

Line a large, lightly greased pie dish
with 4 sheets filo pastry and trim
edges. Fill with spinach and potato
mixture and spread evenly. Top with
2 sheets of filo pastry and trim edges.
Lightly wipe over top with water,
using a pastry brush. Sprinkle with
sesame seeds or poppy seeds. Cook at
220°C for 10 minutes. Turn heat
down to 200°C and cook for a further
20 minutes.

POTATO AND CORN CROQUETTES

Makes 6

500 g potato, peeled
1 onion, diced
2 teaspoons grain mustard
200 g cooked corn kernels, puréed
1 egg white
100 g carrot, grated
2 tablespoons finely chopped fresh
    parsley
2 egg whites mixed with 1 tablespoon
    water
1½ cups wholemeal breadcrumbs or
    oat bran or a combination of both

Boil or steam potato until tender.
Drain. Add onion, mustard, corn, egg
white, carrot and parsley. Mix together
well. Form into 6 croquettes and
refrigerate until firm to handle. Dip
croquettes in the egg white and water
mixture and roll in the breadcrumbs.

Grease a non-stick pan with a little
light olive oil. Gently cook, turning to
brown all sides, for approximately
15–20 minutes, or place on a non-
stick baking tray and cook, in an oven
preheated to 180°C, for 30 minutes or
until browned and crisp on all sides.

NOT QUITE IRISH (POTATO) STEW

Serves 8–10

1 kg potato

1 sweet potato (orange), approximately 200 g

1 parsnip, approximately 125 g

2 medium carrots, approximately 200 g

1 zucchini, approximately 250 g

2 medium onions, quartered

3 cups boiling water

1 tablespoon Vecon

1 × 375 ml can salt-free vegetable juice

2 cups frozen peas

¼ cup finely chopped fresh parsley

3 tablespoons cornflour

¼ cup water

Preheat oven to 190°C.

Prepare vegetables by peeling and cutting into cubes. Potato cubes should be twice the size of other vegetables. In a large ovenproof dish dissolve 1 tablespoon Vecon in 1 cup boiling water. Add all vegetables except peas. Cover with remaining water and vegetable juice. Cover and cook for about 40 minutes in the oven.

When vegetables are just tender, add peas, parsley and combined cornflour and water. Cook for 5 minutes more after stew has come to the boil again. Serve with wholemeal bread.

PUMPKIN BEAN BAKE

Serves 2
2 small orange baby pumpkins
1 cup Quick and Easy Tomato Sauce
(see page 58)
1 × 310 g can red kidney beans,
rinsed
2 tablespoons finely chopped fresh
parsley
2 tablespoons finely chopped chives

Preheat oven to 200°C.

Cut tops off pumpkins. Scoop out
seeds and discard. Cut away pumpkin
flesh to create a firm outer shell. Chop
up pumpkin flesh finely. Add this to
beans, tomato sauce and herbs. Spoon
mixture back into pumpkins. Place lids
on. Put pumpkins in a shallow dish
and cover. Bake in oven for 50
minutes or until pumpkins are very
tender.

EGG COMBINATION RICE

Serves 6
3 whole eggs (if any member of the
family has high cholesterol, it may
be best to avoid using egg yolks)
¼ cup low-fat milk or low-fat soy
milk
1 medium onion, chopped
1 clove garlic, crushed
½ teaspoon finely chopped fresh
ginger
125 g red capsicum, diced
125 g green capsicum, diced
125 g carrot, diced
125 g zucchini, diced
1 tablespoon water
pinch of cumin powder
pinch of coriander powder
pinch of chilli powder
1 tablespoon low-salt soy sauce
4 cups cooked rice

Beat eggs and soy milk together until
light and fluffy. Pour onto a large, hot,
lightly greased, non-stick frypan. Turn
to cook the other side. It is cooked
when firm and yellow in colour. Do
not allow to brown. Remove from pan
and chop up into small pieces. Clean
away egg from pan.

Add onion, garlic, ginger, vegetables and water to pan. Toss vegetables well and add spices. Cook for 3 minutes. Turn heat up to high. Add rice, a cup at a time, and mix to combine vegetables evenly. Keep turning, using an egg lifter so the rice does not stick to the bottom of the pan. Add egg and mix through rice. When heated through, rice is ready to eat.

SWEET POTATO AND LENTIL BURGERS

Makes 6
½ cup uncooked brown lentils
100 g carrot, peeled
400 g sweet potato, peeled
1 onion, peeled and diced
2 teaspoons low-salt soy sauce
2 tablespoons finely chopped fresh
    parsley or chives
ground black pepper to taste
½ cup oat bran

Yoghurt Curry Dressing
1 cup non-fat or low-fat yoghurt
1 teaspoon curry powder
1 teaspoon cumin powder

Boil lentils until soft (about 30–40 minutes), and drain. Cook carrot, sweet potato and onion together until vegetables are soft. Drain. Mash carrot, sweet potato and onion. Add lentils, soy sauce, parsley and black pepper to taste. Shape into 6 burgers and press into oat bran to coat lightly.

Cook in a non-stick pan to brown on both sides. Serve with yoghurt curry dressing.

To make the dressing, combine all ingredients. Mix well and store in a covered container in refrigerator.

SPINACH AND COTTAGE CHEESE CANNELLONI

Serves 4

8 cannelloni shells
200 g low-fat cottage cheese
1 teaspoon grated Parmesan cheese
2 tablespoons chopped chives
150 g cooked, well-drained spinach (a
   250 g box of frozen spinach yields
   150 g well-drained spinach)
pinch of nutmeg
1 egg white

Tomato Sauce

½ onion, diced
1 teaspoon crushed garlic
½ cup dry white wine
1 × 425 g can salt-free tomatoes,
   crushed
1 × 140 ml tub tomato paste
1 tablespoon fresh chopped basil or
   ½ teaspoon dried basil
1 tablespoon fresh chopped chives

Preheat oven to 180°C.

Combine all cannelloni filling ingredients. Mix well and spoon into shells.

To make the sauce, sauté onion and garlic over low heat until onion begins to soften. Add wine and remaining ingredients. Simmer uncovered for 20 minutes. Place cannelloni in a shallow casserole dish and pour over sauce. Cover and cook in oven for 30 minutes. (Portions of this recipe can be frozen and reheated in the microwave oven.)

SPINACH AND POTATO PASTIES

Makes 8

Pastry

1 cup unbleached wholemeal plain
  flour
1 cup unbleached white plain flour
½ cup unbleached wholemeal self-
  raising flour
3 tablespoons light olive oil
1 tablespoon lemon juice
1 cup cold water
extra flour for kneading

Filling

600 g potato, peeled and diced
1 onion, peeled and finely diced
1 cup frozen peas
100 g spinach, finely chopped
1 tablespoon tomato paste
1 tablespoon low-salt soy sauce
1 tablespoon grated Parmesan cheese
1 egg white combined with a little
  water

To make the pastry, sift the flours into a large bowl, and add the husks. Make a well in the middle of the flour and add oil and lemon juice. Work through the flour with your fingertips. Gradually add water. Mix well until mixture comes together to make a ball. Knead lightly on a floured board. Chill for about 30 minutes in the refrigerator.

While the pastry is chilling, preheat oven to 180°C and prepare the filling. Steam potatoes until just tender. Run them under cold water and drain well. Add onions and frozen peas. Steam the spinach until soft, then squeeze any moisture from it and add it to the potato mixture. Stir in the tomato paste, soy sauce and cheese.

Take the pastry and cut it into 8 equal portions. Roll out each portion into a circle. Divide the filling between the circles. Wipe around the edge of the pastry with the combined egg white and water. Fold the pastry over to make half-circles. Cut small air holes in the pastry for steam to escape. Place on a baking tray and cook for 30 minutes.

TOMATO CHEESE QUICHE

Serves 4–6

Base

3 cups wholemeal breadcrumbs

2 tablespoons salt-free tomato juice

Filling

1 medium onion, diced

1 × 425 g can salt-free tomatoes

½ teaspoon dried basil

½ teaspoon dried oregano

½ teaspoon coriander powder

400 g low-fat ricotta cheese

4 egg whites

2 large tomatoes

1 cup finely grated low-fat grating
   cheese

Preheat oven to 180°C.

Combine base ingredients and press firmly into a 22-cm round lightly greased pie dish. Bake for 10–15 minutes or until lightly browned. Remove from oven and leave to cool.

For the filling, turn oven up to 220°C to preheat. Cook onion in a little water until soft (approximately 2–3 minutes). Remove from heat, add tomatoes, basil, oregano, coriander and ricotta cheese. Purée until very smooth. Beat egg whites until light and fluffy and gently fold into tomato mixture.

Pour the mixture over the cooked breadcrumb base. Carefully lay slices of tomato on top to cover and spread cheese evenly over the tomato. Cook at 220°C for 15 minutes and turn down to 190°C for a further 30 minutes.

Garnish with extra slices of tomato and fresh parsley. Delicious either hot or cold.

SWEET AND SOUR VEGETABLES

Serves 6–8

2 tablespoons salt-free tomato paste

2 tablespoons low-salt soy sauce

1 teaspoon finely chopped fresh
  ginger

¾ cup unsweetened pineapple juice

¼ cup white wine vinegar

1¼ cups Chinese chicken stock (see
  page 64)

1 small onion, sliced into rings

200 g carrot, cut diagonally and in
  half again

200 g celery, cut diagonally

200 g zucchini, cut into small chunks

200 g mushrooms, sliced

1 medium red capsicum, chopped

1 medium green capsicum, chopped

1 × 440 g can unsweetened
  pineapple pieces

1 tablespoon and 1 teaspoon
  cornflour

6 spring onions, diagonally sliced

Add the first 5 ingredients to a cold
wok with ¼ cup of stock. Slowly bring
to the boil and simmer covered for
1 minute. Add onions, carrot, celery
and zucchini. Toss to combine
ingredients. Cook, covered, for
2 minutes.

Add mushrooms and capsicums. Toss
to combine all ingredients. Cook,
covered, for another 2 minutes.

Add pineapple pieces and combined
remaining stock and cornflour. Wait
for sauce to boil and cook, covered,
for a further 3 minutes. Serve
immediately, garnished with spring
onions.

EGG-YOLK VEGETABLE OMELETTE

Serves 1

1 egg
1 extra egg white
½ cup low-fat milk or low-fat soy
  milk
50 g carrot, grated
50 g zucchini, grated
50 g fresh tomato, chopped
50 g low-fat grating cheese, grated

Beat egg and egg white with soy milk until light and fluffy. Fold in vegetables. Pour onto a hot, lightly greased, non-stick frypan. Spread vegetables evenly over omelette. Sprinkle cheese over the top. Cook for a few minutes until the omelette begins to firm on the bottom then place under a griller until cheese and top brown. Fold in half and remove from pan. Serve with a salad.

VEGETABLE SPRING ROLLS

Makes 8

8 sheets filo pastry
1 egg white
2 tablespoons cornflour
¼ cup water
1 teaspoon curry powder

Filling

1 teaspoon fresh finely grated ginger
½ red capsicum, finely diced
4 shallots, finely chopped
5 medium mushrooms, finely chopped
1 cup wholemeal breadcrumbs
400 g cabbage, finely shredded
1 tablespoon dry sherry
1 tablespoon low-salt soy sauce

Preheat oven to 190°C.

Combine all filling ingredients and mix well with hands. Combine egg white, cornflour, water and curry powder and make a thin paste.

To assemble, fold a filo sheet in half. Brush lightly with cornflour mixture. Take a handful of filling and place it evenly across one corner of the filo sheet. Roll up in an envelope-shape, making sure edges have been brushed with the cornflour mixture. Place on a non-stick baking tray. Repeat with remaining mixture. Bake for 30–40 minutes.

ZUCCHINI STUFFED WITH CHILLI BEANS

Serves 6

3 large zucchini
1 quantity chilli beans (see below)
1 cup wholemeal breadcrumbs
1 cup grated low-fat grating cheese

Chilli Beans

100 g Aduki beans
1 × 425 g can salt-free tomatoes and juice
2 small red chillies (for a milder flavour use a red capsicum)
2 spring onions, finely chopped
1 clove garlic, crushed
¼ teaspoon cumin powder
¼ teaspoon dried oregano
2 tablespoons salt-free tomato paste

Soak beans overnight. Drain and discard any beans that have not absorbed the water. Place in a clean saucepan and cover with water. Bring to the boil. Reduce heat, cover and simmer for 1–1½ hours or until beans are tender. Drain and set aside.

Chop tomatoes and put in pan with juice. Add very finely chopped chillies, spring onions, garlic, spices and tomato paste. Cook for 15 minutes, stirring occasionally.

Cut zucchini in half lengthwise and scoop out seeds and some flesh. Chop flesh finely and add to tomato mixture. Cook a further 5 minutes. Add beans and keep hot.

Preheat oven to 210°C.

Lightly steam zucchini shells until just tender. Fill zucchini with bean mixture. Place in a non-stick casserole. Sprinkle over breadcrumbs and the cheese. Bake for 15 minutes.

ZUCCHINI, CHEESE AND OAT BRAN PANCAKES

Makes 8

1 cup rolled oats
½ cup oat bran
1 cup unbleached white plain flour
2 teaspoons baking powder
2 cups grated raw zucchini (firmly packed and squeezed to remove all excess liquid)
¼ cup firmly packed grated low-fat grating cheese
1 cup evaporated skim milk
1 cup water
2 egg whites
black pepper to taste

White Sauce

1 cup low-fat milk or low-fat soy milk
2 tablespoons cornflour
black pepper to taste

In a large bowl combine rolled oats and bran. Sift the flour and baking powder over the oats and combine. Add zucchini and cheese and mix.

Opposite
Chinese Corn and Vegetable
Combination (see page 64).

Combine milk and water and stir through the flour and zucchini mixture. Beat egg whites until stiff and gently fold through the batter. Cook on a lightly greased pancake pan until browned on both sides.

Top these pancakes with avocado and alfalfa sprouts and a low-fat mayonnaise (see page 27) and roll up. Or make a basic white sauce and add chopped cooked chicken, left-over fish, salmon or cooked vegetables and use as a filling.

To make the white sauce, pour all but 2 tablespoons milk into a saucepan and bring to the boil. Mix cornflour with remaining milk until smooth. Just as bubbles appear prior to boiling, add the cornflour paste and beat well. Season with black pepper.

Variations

Add to the basic white sauce one of the following:
- 2 tablespoons grated low-fat cheese
- 2 tablespoons chopped chives
- 1 tablespoon chopped parsley
- 2 teaspoons Dijon mustard.

Opposite
Carob Mousse (see page 88).

ZUCCHINI MOUSSAKA

Serves 6–8
600 g large zucchini, thinly sliced
1 cup grated low-fat grating cheese

Tomato Sauce
1 onion, finely diced
2 cloves garlic, crushed
250 g carrot, finely diced
250 g mushrooms, finely diced
3 bay leaves
1 teaspoon dried oregano
1 teaspoon dried basil
2 × 425 g cans salt-free tomatoes
   and juice
¼ cup salt-free tomato paste

White Sauce
500 ml low-fat milk or low-fat soy
   milk
4 tablespoons cornflour
dash of cayenne pepper
1 tablespoon skim-milk herb cheese

Preheat oven to 190°C.

Boil or steam zucchini until just tender and drain. Set aside.

To make the tomato sauce, cook onion and garlic in 2 tablespoons water until soft and transparent. Add remaining ingredients except tomato

paste and simmer, covered, for
15 minutes. Remove bay leaves and
chop up tomatoes using a wooden
spoon. Add tomato paste. Turn heat
up and cook, uncovered, until sauce
thickens, stirring occasionally.

To make the white sauce, place soy
milk in saucepan, reserving ¼ cup.
Blend reserved milk with cornflour to
make a paste. Bring milk in pan to
almost boiling and stir in cayenne
pepper and skim-milk herb cheese.
Add cornflour paste and stir
continuously until sauce thickens.

Lightly grease an oblong ovenproof
dish with high sides. Place a layer of
zucchini on the base of the dish. Place
over a layer of tomato sauce, enough
to spread and cover zucchini. Repeat
with alternate layers of zucchini and
sauce. Top with layer of white sauce,
and sprinkle with grated cheese. Bake
for 20–30 minutes or until cheese has
melted and is brown and bubbling.

VEGETARIAN DELIGHT PIZZA

Makes 2 large pita breads
2 cups pizza sauce (see below)
**200 g low-fat grating cheese, finely
    grated**
**200 g carrots, cut into thin rounds
    and lightly cooked until just soft**
**200 g zucchini, cut into thin rounds
    and lightly cooked until just soft**
**150 g tomato, cut into thin round
    slices**

Pizza Sauce
Makes approximately 5 cups
3 medium onions, diced
2 cloves garlic, crushed
**2 × 400 g cans salt-free tomatoes,
    puréed**
1 cup salt-free tomato paste
½ teaspoon dried basil
1 teaspoon dried oregano

To make the pizza sauce, cook onions
and garlic in a little water until soft.
Add remaining ingredients and boil
for 5 minutes to thicken. Set aside to
cool.

Preheat oven to 200°C.

Spread 1 cup pizza sauce over each
base. Sprinkle cheese over sauce. Place

carrot rounds and zucchini rounds over
cheese. Top with slices of tomato.
Cook for 10–15 minutes. Serve with a
large tossed salad.

Variations

- For a Hawaiian pizza, use 1 cup
  pizza sauce, 75 g each of green and
  red capsicum (cut in strips), 200 g
  unsweetened pineapple chunks and
  50 g low-fat grating cheese, finely
  grated.
- For a mushroom pizza, use 1 cup
  pizza sauce, 200 g finely chopped
  mushrooms and 100 g low-fat
  grating cheese, finely grated.

DESSERTS

APPLE SNOW

Serves 4
4 Granny Smith apples
1 teaspoon lemon juice
1 teaspoon grated lemon rind

Place unpeeled apples in freezer for at least 8 hours. Remove and let stand for 10 minutes. Carefully remove peel and core and cut into chunks. Toss in the lemon juice and lemon rind. Place in a food processor and process using steel blade until light and fluffy.

Serve in cups with spoons or mix with kiwi fruit. Alternatively, cut a pear in half and remove core and some of the flesh. Wipe over with lemon juice and freeze for 1 hour. Scoop the apple snow onto the pear. Garnish with blueberries, kiwi fruit or fresh strawberries.

BANANA CUSTARD

Serves 6–8
3–4 bananas
1 tablespoon lemon juice

Custard
4 cups low-fat milk or low-fat soy milk
1 cup cornflour
2 teaspoons vanilla essence
1 tablespoon grated orange rind
¼–½ cup apple juice concentrate
1 cup non-fat yoghurt

To make the custard, bring 3 cups of milk to just below boiling. Combine 1 cup of milk, cornflour, vanilla and orange rind and mix to make a paste. Add to milk and stir briskly until thick. Cook for 2 minutes, stirring continuously. Remove from heat. Add apple juice concentrate and mix well. Add yoghurt and mix well.

Cut bananas into thin rounds and brush with lemon juice. Line a shallow baking dish with foil or plastic wrap (for easy removal). Overlap banana pieces on base of dish. Pour over custard. Refrigerate to set for at least 3 hours. Turn out and cut into squares. Top with low-fat cream.

BLUEBERRY YOGHURT SWIRL

Serves 1–2
1 cup non-fat yoghurt
½ cup blueberry sauce
handful of fresh blueberries

Blueberry Sauce

1¾ cups unsweetened natural pear
   juice
⅓ cup apple juice concentrate
1 tablespoon lemon juice
2 teaspoons agar powder
450 g fresh blueberries

To make the blueberry sauce, combine pear juice, lemon juice, apple juice concentrate and agar in a small saucepan. Bring to the boil. Boil for 5 minutes, stirring continuously. Add blueberries and boil for 10 minutes.

Place ½ cup blueberry sauce in the bottom of a tall glass. Add yoghurt. Using a long-handled spoon, swirl blueberry sauce through yoghurt. Top with fresh blueberries and serve chilled.

Extra blueberry sauce can be poured into sterilised jars, and kept refrigerated. Use on pancakes, in muffins and on toast.

CANTALOUP BERRY BASKET

Serves 3
1 cantaloup
2–3 cups mixed berries, such as
   boysenberries, blueberries,
   raspberries, loganberries,
   blackberries or strawberries

Cut cantaloup into quarters. Remove seeds and scoop out the flesh to make a basket-like hollow. Use a sharp knife to remove the flesh carefully from one quarter, leaving approximately 1 cm orange flesh. Cut up the removed flesh into pieces.

Cut the outer skin into three long strips which will become the basket handles. Attach these to either end of remaining pieces of cantaloup using toothpicks. Wash berries and drain. Fill baskets. Serve with home-made ice-cream or non-fat yoghurt.

CAROB MOUSSE

Serves 6

4 cups low-fat milk or low-fat soy
  milk
1 cup cornflour
2 teaspoons vanilla essence
½ cup carob powder
4 tablespoons boiling water
1 tablespoon grated orange rind
½ teaspoon orange essence
1 cup non-fat yoghurt
4 egg whites
strawberries

Place 3 cups of milk in a large
saucepan and bring to just below
boiling. Add reserved cup of milk to
cornflour and mix to a smooth paste.
Add vanilla.

Combine the carob with the boiling
water and mix to a paste to dissolve
the carob. Add orange rind and
orange essence. Combine cornflour
and carob. Add this to the heating
milk and stir continuously until sauce
thickens. Remove from heat and fold
through yoghurt.

Beat egg whites until stiff peaks form.
Gently fold egg whites through the
mixture. Pour into a mould or
individual glasses. Refrigerate for at
least 2 hours. Serve topped with fresh
strawberries.

APPLE MINT JELLY

Serves 4

2 cups unsweetened apple juice

1 teaspoon agar powder

1–2 teaspoons finely chopped fresh
mint or spearmint

Boil 1 teaspoon of agar with 1 cup
apple juice for 3 minutes or until agar
has dissolved. Stir briskly into
remaining cold juice. Stir continuously
for 3 minutes. Stir through the mint.
Refrigerate to set.

BERRY SUMMER JELLY PUDDING

Serves 8

800 g berries in season (combination
of strawberries, blueberries,
raspberries, red currants, cherries)

4 cups water

4 teaspoons agar powder

¼ cup apple juice concentrate

Clean berries, removing stems. Cut
strawberries in half. Remove pips from
cherries and cut in half.

Place the last 3 ingredients in a
saucepan and bring to the boil.
Simmer for 3–5 minutes or until agar
is dissolved. Turn up heat and add
berries. Stir carefully. Bring nearly to
the boil. Fruit will begin to bleed their
colours into the liquid and just begin
to break open. Do not overcook them.

Remove from heat and pour into a
round pudding bowl to set. Refrigerate
to firm. Cut into wedges to serve.

BLUEBERRY GRAPE JELLY

Serves 6
2 cups dark unsweetened grape juice
2 teaspoons agar powder
2 cups blueberries, fresh or frozen

Boil 2 teaspoons agar with 1 cup juice
and blueberries for 3 minutes or until
agar has dissolved. Stir briskly into
remaining cold juice. Stir continuously
for 3 minutes. Refrigerate to set.

MANGO AND PEACH JELLY LOG

Serves 6–8
2 mangoes, peeled
6 yellow peaches, peeled (mangoes
    and peaches together should weigh
    approximately 700 g)
2 passionfruit
1 cup water
1 tablespoon apple juice concentrate
2 teaspoons agar powder
1 cup fresh orange juice (freshly
    squeezed and sieved to remove
    small fibres)

Chop fruit into bite-sized pieces and
add passionfruit pulp.

Combine water, apple juice
concentrate and agar powder in a
saucepan. Slowly bring to the boil,
stirring continuously until agar
dissolves. Remove from heat, add
orange juice. Pour over fruit
immediately and spoon into a long
glass terrine-style dish. Refrigerate
until firm, then cut into slices. (The
log keeps well if refrigerated and well
covered.)

LEMON PEAR SORBET

Serves 8–10

1 × 825 g can unsweetened pears
  and juice
¼ cup apple juice concentrate
4 tablespoons lemon juice

Purée all ingredients. Pour into an
ice-cream maker and follow freezing
instructions. Serve in sugar-free
ice-cream cones. Garnish with a piece
of fresh fruit such as a strawberry or
kiwi fruit.

LEMON PARFAIT

Serves 4–6

1 teaspoon gelatine
2 tablespoons boiling water
1 cup evaporated skim milk, ice-cold
1 cup lemon pancake topping (see
  page 9)

Dissolve gelatine in boiling water and
set aside to cool. Beat milk until thick
and at least doubled in size. Beat in
the lemon pancake topping. (If lemon
pancake topping has been refrigerated
you will need to heat it slightly to
soften the texture and ensure easier
combining.) Add gelatine and pour
into parfait glasses and refrigerate.
Garnish with green and purple grapes
and a mint leaf.

LEMON 'MERINGUE' PIE

Serves 8

Pastry

1 cup unbleached wholemeal plain
  flour
1 cup rolled oats
¼ cup cold pressed grapeseed oil
2 tablespoons apple juice concentrate
4 tablespoons lemon juice

Lemon Filling

¾ cup lemon juice
½ cup apple juice concentrate
grated rind of 1 orange
  (approximately 1 tablespoon)
grated rind of 1 lemon (approximately
  1 tablespoon)
1¼ cups water
½ cup cornflour

Meringue

4 egg whites
100 g almonds, finely ground
1 teaspoon vanilla essence
2 tablespoons apple juice concentrate

Preheat oven to 220°C.

Combine all pastry ingredients in a
food processor and process until pastry
binds together. Roll out to fit a
medium fluted pie dish. Cook at
220°C for 10–15 minutes. Cool.

To make the lemon filling, place the
first 4 ingredients plus 1 cup water in
a small saucepan and bring to the boil.
Combine ¼ cup water with cornflour
and make into a paste. Stir into lemon
mixture stirring continuously as it
boils and thickens. Cook for
2 minutes. Cool slightly. Pour into
base and leave to set.

The lemon filling should be quite cold
and firm before making the meringue
topping.

For the meringue, preheat oven to
200°C and beat egg whites until stiff
peaks form. Add all other ingredients
separately, mixing well after each
addition. Spoon over lemon filling.
Bake for 10–15 minutes or until top
has browned.

This pie should be kept out of the
refrigerator for best flavour. Serve with
non-fat frozen yoghurt or home-made
ice-cream.

PEACH YOGHURT MOUSSE

1 × 825 g can unsweetened peaches,
   drained
2 tablespoons apple juice concentrate
½ teaspoon orange essence
1 tablespoon gelatine
3 tablespoons boiling water
1½–2 cups non-fat yoghurt

Blend peaches, apple juice concentrate
and orange essence in a blender.
Dissolve gelatine in boiling water and
add to peach mixture. Fold in the
yoghurt. Pour into a wet mould and
refrigerate until set. Serve with fresh
strawberries and slices of fresh peaches.

PINEAPPLE FRUIT BOAT

Serves 1–2
1 small fresh pineapple
some fresh strawberries
some banana, chopped
some Jonathan or Delicious apple,
   roughly chopped
1 passionfruit

Cut pineapple, including green foliage,
in half. Cut out pineapple flesh and
remove the core. Chop up pineapple
flesh finely. Combine all other
ingredients and toss well in the
passionfruit pulp. Spoon into the
pineapple shell and refrigerate well.
Delicious served with frozen non-fat
yoghurt.

RASPBERRY SOUFFLÉ

Serves 6

1 cup raspberries (fresh or frozen) or combination of raspberries and blueberries
2 teaspoons apple juice concentrate
1 cup evaporated skim milk, well chilled
1 teaspoon vanilla essence
1 tablespoon gelatine
¼ cup boiling water

Place berries in a saucepan with apple juice concentrate. Gently heat to soften the berries. Cool slightly.

Beat milk until doubled in size and quite thick. Add berries and continue to beat. Add vanilla essence.

Dissolve gelatine in boiling water. Add to the milk mixture while still beating.

Pour into a small soufflé bowl. The height can be extended by wrapping foil around the top of the soufflé bowl. Refrigerate to set for at least 2 hours before serving. Serve with fresh berries.

ORANGE, CANTALOUP AND PASSIONFRUIT CUPS

Serves 4

4 oranges
¼–½ small cantaloup
4 passionfruit
½ cup unsweetened orange juice

Remove tops from oranges and carefully scoop out orange flesh. Remove white pith and pips and chop orange finely. Cut up cantaloup finely. Scoop pulp from passionfruit. Combine fruits and orange juice. Spoon into orange cups and chill.

STRAWBERRY AND PASSIONFRUIT TOPPED PAVLOVA

Serves 12
10 dried apricots
½ cup unsweetened orange juice
1 × 375 ml can evaporated skim
   milk, well chilled
1 teaspoon vanilla essence
1 tablespoon apple juice concentrate
1 teaspoon white wine vinegar
1 tablespoon gelatine
½ cup boiling water
2 cups low-fat whipped cream
3 cups strawberries, washed and
   hulled
¼ cup passionfruit pulp

Simmer apricots in orange juice for
10 minutes or until soft. Purée. Beat
milk until thick and at least doubled
in size. Blend in apricots, vanilla,
apple juice concentrate and vinegar.
Dissolve gelatine in boiling water and
fold into mixture. Pour into a round,
spring-form cheesecake tin. Refrigerate
until firm. Top with cream,
strawberries and passionfruit pulp.

STRAWBERRY CUSTARD PARFAIT

Serves 6
1 quantity of custard (see page 96)
6 cups hulled strawberries

Make custard and let cool slightly.
Cut strawberries into quarters.
Alternate layers of strawberries and
custard in a parfait glass. Decorate the
top with sliced strawberries.
Refrigerate when custard has
completely set.

STRAWBERRY CUSTARD TARTS

Makes 8

2 cups strawberries, washed and
hulled

Pastry

1 cup unbleached wholemeal plain
flour
1 cup rolled oats
¼ cup cold pressed grapeseed oil
2 tablespoons apple juice concentrate
2–4 tablespoons unsweetened orange
juice

Custard

2 cups low-fat milk or low-fat soy
milk
½ cup cornflour
1 teaspoon vanilla essence
1 tablespoon grated orange rind
2–3 tablespoons apple juice
concentrate
½ cup non-fat yoghurt

Preheat oven to 210°C.

Lightly grease 8 small foil pie plates, 8 cm × 2 cm. Combine all ingredients for pastry in a food processor. Using the steel blade, process until pastry binds together. Cut pastry into 8 equal pieces and roll out to fit the pie plates. Trim edges and place on a baking tray. Cook for 10 minutes. Cool.

To make the custard, bring 1½ cups milk to just below boiling point in a medium saucepan. Combine rest of milk with the cornflour, vanilla and orange rind to make a paste. Add to milk and stir briskly until thick. Cook for 2 minutes, stirring continuously. Remove from heat. Add apple juice concentrate and mix well, then add yoghurt and mix well. Cool slightly.

Pour custard into shells. Refrigerate. Decorate the tops with fresh strawberries.

FRUIT SALAD

Fruit salad can be a nutrituous finish to a meal, served for breakfast or as a snack meal. It need never become boring if you change the combinations of the fruit and soak it in a little juice. Serve plain, with home-made ice-cream, custard or non-fat yoghurt.

Some fruit combinations

- Orange segments, grapefruit segments, pineapple chunks, passionfruit pulp and orange juice.
- Strawberries, watermelon balls and sparkling apple juice.
- Cantaloup balls, honeydew melon balls, green grapes, grated fresh ginger root and natural, unsweetened pear juice.
- Banana chunks, pineapple chunks, apple chunks, purple grapes, lemon juice and natural, unsweetened apple juice.
- Honeydew melon chunks, cantaloup chunks, pineapple chunks, purple and green grapes, blueberries and dark grape juice.
- Orange chunks, apple chunks, pear chunks, pineapple chunks, strips of dried apricot and orange or apple juice.

- Apricot halves, peach pieces, nectarine pieces and apricot nectar.
- Pineapple chunks, banana chunks, passionfruit pulp and unsweetened pineapple juice.
- Strawberries, kiwi fruit chunks, green grapes, grated rind of orange and lemon and unsweetened orange juice.
- Bananas sliced, kiwi fruit sliced, pineapple wedges, orange segments, water chestnuts thinly sliced, glazed cherries (rinsed to remove sugar) and lemon and orange juice.
- Mango, pineapple, passionfruit pulp, fine strips of dried apricot (optional) and unsweetened orange juice.
- Dark plum halves, blueberries, purple grapes and dark grape juice.
- Watermelon balls, honeydew melon balls, cantaloup balls, sparkling apple juice and lemon juice.
- Mango, pineapple and orange chunks, passionfruit pulp and fresh halved dates.
- Banana chunks, passionfruit pulp and fresh halved dates.

CHUNKY BANANA ICE-CREAM

Serves 8–10

1 × 375 ml can evaporated skim
  milk, ice-cold
3 teaspoons vanilla essence
2 tablespoons lemon juice
4 bananas

Beat milk until thick and creamy and
at least doubled in size. Add vanilla
and lemon juice. Add roughly
chopped bananas and beat lightly.
Pour into ice-cream maker and follow
freezing instructions.

Making ice-cream without an ice-cream maker

- All ingredients used should be
  ice-cold.
- All equipment used should be well
  chilled. Place in freezer for at least
  15 minutes prior to using.
- Pour ice-cream into well-chilled
  metal freezing containers.
- To avoid ice-cream texture
  becoming icy rather than creamy,
  you will need to rebeat it several
  times, just as icicles begin to appear
  around the edges again making sure
  that all equipment is well chilled.
- This ice-cream does not store well
  as it becomes rock hard. Make small
  batches and eat as required.
- Should ice-cream become too hard,
  place in a chilled blender or food
  processor and quickly blend to a
  creamy texture. Eat immediately.

BOYSENBERRY ICE-CREAM

Serves 8

1 × 300 g pack frozen unsweetened
   boysenberries
2 tablespoons apple juice concentrate
1 teaspoon vanilla essence or
   ½ teaspoon orange essence
1½ cups evaporated skim milk or
   1 cup low-fat soy milk

Crush berries with the palm of your
hand. Place in a blender or food
processor. Process until a soft but still
icy consistency, like a sorbet. Pour in
remaining ingredients. Beat until at
least doubled in size. Pour into
ice-cream maker and follow freezing
instructions.

RICH CREAMY CAROB ICE-CREAM

Serves 6

1 × 375 ml can evaporated skim
   milk, ice-cold
¼ cup unsweetened carob powder
¼ cup apple juice concentrate
2 teaspoons vanilla essence

In a large bowl beat milk until thick
and at least doubled in size. Combine
carob, apple juice concentrate and
vanilla to make a thick paste. Add
this mixture to milk while still
beating. Pour into the ice-cream
maker and follow freezing instructions.

Variation

- Add 2 tablespoons finely chopped
  roasted almonds, toasted coconut or
  finely chopped raisins.

RICH CREAMY CUSTARD ICE-CREAM

Serves 10
4 cups low-fat milk or low-fat soy
   milk
¼ cup cornflour
1 tablespoon grated orange rind
2 teaspoons vanilla essence
½ cup apple juice concentrate
1 cup non-fat yoghurt or low-fat
   milk, extra

Place 3 cups of milk in a saucepan
and slowly bring to the boil. Combine
cornflour, orange rind and vanilla with
reserved cup of milk. Stir to make a
smooth paste. Add to hot milk and
stir continuously for 2–3 minutes,
until the mixture thickens. Remove
from heat. Add apple juice
concentrate and fold through. Add
yoghurt or milk and stir again until
smooth. Cool until just warm. Pour
into ice-cream maker and follow
freezing instructions.

ORANGE-FLAVOURED ICE-CREAM

Serves 6
1 × 375 ml can evaporated skim
   milk, ice-cold
2 teaspoons vanilla essence
1 teaspoon orange essence
¼ cup apple juice concentrate

In a large bowl beat milk until thick
and at least doubled in size. Add
remaining ingredients while still
beating. Pour into ice-cream maker
and follow freezing instructions.

PASSIONFRUIT ICE-CREAM

Serves 6

½ × 375 ml can evaporated skim
milk, ice-cold
1 cup unsweetened fruit juice
cocktail (a combination of apple,
orange, peach and passionfruit
juices)
½ teaspoon orange essence
¼ cup apple juice concentrate
2 tablespoons passionfruit pulp

Beat milk in a large bowl until thick
and at least doubled in size. Add
remaining ingredients except passionfruit while still beating. Pour into
ice-cream maker and follow freezing
instructions. When ice-cream begins
to thicken, add passionfruit pulp.

PINEAPPLE-FLAVOURED ICE-CREAM

Serves 10–12

1 × 375 ml can evaporated skim
milk, ice-cold
2 teaspoons vanilla essence
2 cups unsweetened pineapple juice
½ cup apple juice concentrate

Beat milk in a large bowl until thick
and at least doubled in size. Add
remaining ingredients while still
beating. Pour into ice-cream maker
and follow freezing instructions.

STRAWBERRY ICE-CREAM

Serves 8–10

1 × 375 ml can evaporated skim
  milk, ice-cold
2 teaspoons vanilla essence
1 tablespoon apple juice concentrate
2 punnets strawberries

In a large bowl beat milk until thick
and creamy and at least doubled in
size. Add vanilla and apple juice
concentrate. Mash 1 punnet of
strawberries and cut remaining
strawberries in half. Add strawberries.
Pour into ice-cream maker and follow
freezing instructions.

FROZEN YOGHURT ICE-CREAM

3 cups non-fat yoghurt
2 tablespoons apple juice concentrate
1–2 teaspoons vanilla essence

Combine all ingredients. Pour into an
ice-cream maker and follow freezing
instructions.

If you don't have an ice-cream maker,
pour into a stainless steel bowl and
place in freezer. As yoghurt freezes
around the edge of the bowl, stir the
frozen particles into the mixture.
Continue to do this until yoghurt is
frozen. It should be served more as a
soft-serve dessert than a hard
ice-cream. Do not beat the yoghurt as
the texture will easily separate.

CAKES, SLICES AND COOKIES

APPLE AND DATE BARS

Makes approximately 24 bars

Pastry

2 cups unbleached wholemeal plain
   flour
2 cups rolled oats
½ cup cold pressed grapeseed oil
¼ cup apple juice concentrate
½ cup unsweetened orange juice or
   ½ unsweetened orange juice and
   ½ lemon juice

Filling

250 g dates, finely chopped
2 Granny Smith apples, peeled, cored
   and sliced
1 cup unsweetened orange juice
1 teaspoon finely grated orange rind

Preheat oven to 180°C.

Combine flour and oats in a food processor and process lightly. Add oil and apple juice concentrate and orange juice. Process until pastry binds together. Divide in half. Roll out pastry to make two rectangles. One should be approximately 20 cm × 30 cm, the other slightly bigger. Place the larger piece of pastry on the base of a 20 cm × 30 cm foil-lined slice tin.

Place all filling ingredients in a small saucepan. Simmer for 20 minutes or until mixture is soft and most of the orange juice absorbed. Cool slightly.

Pour over base and spread evenly. Carefully cover with the top piece of pastry so that it does not break. Press down at the edges to meet the bottom layer. Bake for 20–30 minutes. Cool in tin before cutting into bars.

APPLE AND DATE CAKE (EGG-FREE)

Serves 12

2½ cups unbleached wholemeal plain
  flour
3 teaspoons baking powder
1 teaspoon cinnamon
1 teaspoon mixed spice
1 teaspoon finely grated lemon rind
3 medium Granny Smith apples,
  peeled and finely diced
1 cup dates, finely chopped
1 teaspoon vanilla essence
¼ cup cold pressed grapeseed oil
½ cup non-fat yoghurt or non-fat
  buttermilk
½ cup apple juice concentrate

Preheat oven to 180°C.

Sift dry ingredients twice into a large
bowl. Add lemon, apple and dates.
Coat well with the flour. Combine
vanilla, oil, yoghurt and apple juice
concentrate. Add to other ingredients
and mix well. Spoon into a foil-lined
20-cm round cake tin. Bake for 50–60
minutes or until firm to touch on top
and an inserted skewer comes out dry.
Cool in tin. Decorate with thin slices
of red and green apple.

APRICOT AND ALMOND HEALTH CHEWS

½ cup dried apricots, chopped
¼ cup unsweetened orange juice
2 tablespoons apple juice concentrate
½ cup skim milk powder
¼ cup whole almonds, roughly
  chopped
1 tablespoon sesame seeds, toasted
1 teaspoon grated orange rind
½ cup sultanas or currants
¼ cup shredded coconut
extra shredded coconut, toasted

Place apricots, orange juice and apple
juice concentrate in a saucepan and
simmer over low heat for 10 minutes.
Do not drain. Remove saucepan from
heat. Blend in skim milk powder. Add
almonds, sesame seeds, grated orange
rind, sultanas and coconut. Mix well
and leave to cool slightly.

Roll mixture into a log shape and roll
in toasted coconut. Roll up in foil and
keep in refrigerator. Cut into rounds
as required. Wrap individual pieces in
coloured cellophane to use as gifts.

APRICOT LOAF (EGG-FREE)

Makes 10–12 slices

1 cup bran

1 cup dried apricots, chopped

¾ cup mixed peel or dried nectarines or dried peaches, finely chopped

2 cups low-fat milk or low-fat soy milk

1½ cups unbleached white self-raising flour

½ cup unbleached wholemeal plain flour

Preheat oven to 180°C.

Mix bran, apricots, mixed peel and milk together in a large bowl. Cover and let stand for at least 2 hours.

Sift the flours. Add flour to the apricot mixture in small amounts and mix well. Pour mixture into a 22 cm × 12 cm lined, non-stick loaf tin and bake for 45–60 minutes or until firm to touch.

APRICOT NIBBLES

Makes approximately 20

¾ cup dried apricots

¾ cup shredded coconut

1 teaspoon grated lemon rind

1 teaspoon grated orange rind

1 tablespoon unsweetened orange juice

extra shredded coconut, toasted

Cover apricots with boiling water and stand 10 minutes. Drain off liquid. Mince apricots in a food blender and mix in lightly with the coconut. Add remaining ingredients except toasted coconut. Knead until well blended. If mixture is too dry add more orange juice. If mixture is too wet add more coconut. Shape into small balls and roll in toasted coconut. Refrigerate.

APRICOT CRUMBLE SLICE

Makes 20–24 pieces

Base

1 cup unbleached wholemeal plain
   flour
1 cup rolled oats
¼ cup cold pressed grapeseed oil
2 tablespoons apple juice concentrate

Filling

250 g dried apricots
1 cup water
1 teaspoon finely grated orange rind

Crumble Topping

2 egg whites
125 g almonds, finely ground
1 teaspoon vanilla essence
2 tablespoons apple juice concentrate
2 tablespoons shredded coconut

Combine all base ingredients in a food
processor and process until ingredients
bind together. Firmly press into a
20 cm × 30 cm slice tin. Set aside.

To make the filling, place apricots,
water and orange rind in a saucepan.
Simmer until apricots are soft
(approximately 10–15 minutes). Purée
and cool slightly. Pour over base.

While apricots are cooking preheat
oven to 180°C.

For the crumble topping, beat egg
whites until stiff peaks form. Fold in
all other ingredients in the order they
are listed. Pour over apricot filling.
Bake for 20–25 minutes or until top is
firm and lightly brown.

APRICOT AND APPLE OAT SLICE

Makes approximately 24 pieces
1 cup whole dried apricots
1 cup dried apples
1 cup whole almonds in their skins
1 cup shredded coconut
2 cups rolled oats
2 teaspoons finely grated orange rind
2 teaspoons finely grated lemon rind
2–4 tablespoons unsweetened orange
    juice

Chop apricots and dried apple finely
in a food processor using the steel
blade. While machine is operating,
add almonds, coconut, oats, orange
and lemon rinds. The mixture should
resemble coarse breadcrumbs. Slowly
add unsweetened juice until mixture
just starts to stick together.

Press firmly into a 20 cm × 30 cm
foil-lined slab tin. Use a round shaped
glass to roll mixture down firmly in
the tin. Refrigerate. Cut into squares
or shapes and keep refrigerated.

OAT MUNCHIES

Makes 20–24
2 cups rolled oats
1 cup unbleached wholemeal plain
    flour
1 teaspoon baking powder
½ teaspoon mixed spice
½ teaspoon cinnamon
1 cup mixed dried fruit medley
¼ cup sunflower seeds
½ cup apple juice concentrate
½ cup cold pressed grapeseed oil
2 egg whites, lightly beaten

Preheat oven to 180°C.

Combine the first 7 ingredients in a
large bowl. In a separate bowl carefully
combine the apple concentrate, oil
and egg whites, and then add to the
oat mixture. Mix together until well
combined and sticky. Place
dessertspoonful mounds on a non-stick
baking sheet. Bake for 10–15 minutes
until golden.

Variations
- Substitute 1 cup currants for dried
  fruit medley.
- Substitute ½ cup chopped dates and
  ½ cup chopped dried apple and
  dried fruit medley.

MUESLI MUNCHIES

Makes 20–24

2 cups toasted muesli, sugar-free and
salt-free
1 cup unbleached wholemeal plain
flour
1 teaspoon baking powder
1 teaspoon cinnamon
¾ cup sultanas
½ cup apple juice concentrate
¼ cup cold pressed grapeseed oil
2 egg whites, lightly beaten

Preheat oven to 180°C.

In a large bowl combine first five
ingredients. In another bowl carefully
combine the apple concentrate, oil,
and egg whites, then add to muesli
mixture. Mix until well combined.
Place dessertspoonfuls on a non-stick
baking tray and bake for 10–15
minutes until golden.

CAROB MUESLI BISCUITS

Makes 18

3 cups Yummy Home-made Muesli
(see page 2)
1 cup unbleached wholemeal
self-raising flour
2 tablespoons carob powder
½ cup cold pressed grapeseed oil
½ cup apple juice concentrate
2 egg whites
2 tablespoons almonds (optional)

Preheat oven to 160°C.

In a large bowl, combine muesli, flour
and carob powder. In another bowl
combine oil and apple juice
concentrate. Add to muesli mixture
and mix through well. Beat egg whites
until thick and creamy and fold
through.

Take a handful of mixture and press
onto a non-stick baking tray. Repeat
with remaining mixture. Press loose
almonds into the top of biscuit. Cook
in oven for 12–15 minutes. Cool on a
rack.

BLUEBERRY CAKE

Serves 12

2 cups unbleached wholemeal plain
   flour
3 teaspoons baking powder
1 teaspoon cinnamon
200–250 g blueberries
¼ cup cold pressed grapeseed oil
½ cup apple juice concentrate
¼ cup non-fat buttermilk
2 teaspoons vanilla essence
2 egg whites

Preheat oven to 180°C.

Sift dry ingredients twice into a large
bowl. Add blueberries and toss in flour
to coat well. In another bowl combine
oil, buttermilk, apple concentrate and
vanilla. Add to flour mixture and mix
well. Beat egg whites until stiff peaks
form and fold carefully through the
mixture. Line a 20-cm round cake tin
with baking paper. Spoon mixture into
tin. Bake for 35–40 minutes.

CARROT CAKE WITH LEMON CHEESE TOPPING

Serves 12

2 cups finely grated carrot
1 cup sultanas
1½ teaspoons cinnamon
½ cup unsweetened orange juice
½ cup apple juice concentrate
⅓ cup cold pressed grapeseed oil
1 cup unbleached wholemeal plain
   flour
1 cup unbleached white plain flour
3 teaspoons baking powder
2 egg whites

Lemon Cheese Topping

1 cup cold Lemon Pancake Topping
   (see page 9)
100 g low-fat ricotta cheese

Preheat oven to 180°C.

Place carrot, sultanas, cinnamon,
orange juice and apple juice
concentrate in a large saucepan and
gently bring to the boil. Simmer for
approximately 5–7 minutes or until
sultanas are soft. Remove from heat
and leave to get cold. Add the oil and
mix well. Combine the sifted flours
and baking powder with the carrot
mixture in 2 lots, mixing well. Beat
egg whites until stiff and gently fold

through the mixture. Spoon into a lined ring tin. Bake for 45–50 minutes. Cake should be completely cool before adding the topping.

To make the topping, blend ingredients until smooth and refrigerate until topping is quite firm. Spread evenly over the top of the cake.

GOLLY WOLLY BANANA LOGS

200 g dried banana
100 g dried apple
1 cup almonds in their skins
1 cup rolled oats
½ cup shredded coconut
3 tablespoons apple juice concentrate
squeeze of lemon or orange juice
extra shredded coconut

Chop banana and apple roughly in a food processor using the steel blade. Add almonds, rolled oats and ½ cup coconut. Process until mixture resembles large breadcrumbs.

Add apple juice concentrate. Process lightly. If the mixture is too dry add a squeeze of lemon or orange juice. Mixture will come together in your hands. Roll into log shapes approximately 4–6 cm long. Roll in coconut. Store in the freezer for a chewy texture.

CAROB PEPPERMINT HEDGEHOG BALLS

1 cup dates
1 cup raisins
1 cup whole almonds in their skins
2 cups rolled oats
1 cup shredded coconut
2 tablespoons carob powder
2 teaspoons vanilla essence
½ teaspoon peppermint essence
2 tablespoons apple juice concentrate

Place dates and raisins in food processor and cut into small pieces. Add almonds, rolled oats, coconut and carob powder. Process until mixture resembles breadcrumbs. Add essences and apple juice concentrate. Mixture should now begin to stick together.

Stop motor and check if the texture is correct by taking a small amount in the palm of your hand and rolling up firmly into a ball. If mixture does not bind, add 1 more tablespoon apple juice concentrate or unsweetened orange juice. Mixture should not be too sticky. Roll into small balls and refrigerate until firm. Keep in the freezer and use as required.

Variation

- Omit peppermint essence and press mixture into a 20 cm × 30 cm slice tin. Roll down firmly using a round glass. Refrigerate and cut into slices when firm.

MUESLI FRUIT BARS

Makes 12

2 cups rolled oats

1 cup wholemeal plain flour

1 teaspoon baking powder

½–1 teaspoon mixed spice

½ teaspoon cinnamon

2 cups dried fruit medley (apricots, apples, pears and sultanas)

½ cup sunflower seeds

½ cup apple juice concentrate

¼ cup cold pressed grapeseed oil

3 egg whites, lightly beaten

Preheat oven to 180°C.

In a large bowl, combine the first 7 ingredients and mix well. Stir through the apple juice concentrate and oil. Add egg whites and mix well.

Line a 20 cm × 30 cm slice tin with non-stick baking paper. Press mixture into tin and flatten. Mark 12 bars with sharp knife. Cook at 200°C for 15–20 minutes. Cool. Cut into bars.

PRUNE BARS

Makes approximately 24

⅔ cup prunes, finely chopped

⅓ cup dried apple, finely chopped

1 tablespoon sunflower seeds

1 tablespoon sesame seeds, toasted

½ cup rolled oats or rolled wheat flakes

½ cup raw bran

1 cup almonds in their skins

½ cup skim milk powder

1 tablespoon vanilla essence

⅓ cup unsweetened orange juice

2 teaspoons finely grated lemon rind

Combine the first 8 ingredients in a food processor and chop roughly. Add vanilla and orange juice to bind. Add lemon rind.

Line a 30 cm × 20 cm slab tin with foil and press mixture into it. Refrigerate for at least 4 hours. Cut into bars.

SCONES AND MUFFINS

WHOLEMEAL PLAIN SCONES

Makes approximately 12
250 g unbleached wholemeal plain
   flour
4 teaspoons baking powder
2 tablespoons skim milk powder
2 tablespoons apple juice concentrate
good squeeze of lemon juice
1 cup low-fat milk or low-fat soy
   milk

Preheat oven to 180°C.

Sift dry ingredients into a large bowl.
Add apple juice concentrate and
lemon juice. Rub into flour using
fingers or the blade of a knife. Bind
with milk to make a dough. Lightly
flour a bench top. Gently knead
dough: too much kneading will make
the scones heavy. Cut into shapes.
Place side by side on a non-stick
baking tray. Bake for 10–15 minutes.
Spread with sugar-free jam.

BANANA AND DATE WHOLEMEAL SCONES

Makes approximately 10
2 cups unbleached wholemeal plain
   flour
3 teaspoons baking powder
¼ teaspoon cinnamon
¼ teaspoon mixed spice
1 cup dates, very finely chopped
1 teaspoon finely grated lemon rind
1 small banana, mashed
¾ cup low-fat milk or low-fat soy
   milk
1 teaspoon lemon juice

Preheat oven to 180°C.

Sift dry ingredients twice into a large
bowl. Add dates and lemon rind and
mix through. Combine banana, milk
and lemon juice. Add this to the flour
and date mixture. Mix together and
knead lightly. Cut into desired shapes.
Place on a non-stick baking tray and
bake for 10–15 minutes. Eat while still
warm.

HERB SCONES

Makes approximately 10
2 cups unbleached white plain flour
3 teaspoons baking powder
1 tablespoon finely chopped fresh
    chives
1 tablespoon finely chopped fresh
    parsley
1 tablespoon finely chopped fresh
    rosemary or basil
2 tablespoons non-fat yoghurt
good squeeze of lemon juice
    (approximately 1 tablespoon)
½ cup low-fat milk or low-fat soy
    milk

Preheat oven to 180°C.

Sift flour and baking powder into a
large bowl. Add herbs and coat with
flour. Add yoghurt and lemon juice
and mix through until flour resembles
fine breadcrumbs. Add milk and mix
through, using a knife. Place scone
dough on a lightly floured bench and
knead lightly. Cut into desired shapes.
Place on a non-stick baking tray and
bake for 10–15 minutes.

PUMPKIN WHOLEMEAL SCONES

Makes approximately 10
1 cup unbleached wholemeal plain
    flour
1 cup unbleached white plain flour
4 teaspoons baking powder
1 teaspoon nutmeg
½ cup lightly packed grated raw
    pumpkin
2 tablespoons non-fat yoghurt
good squeeze of lemon juice
    (approximately 1 tablespoon)
2 teaspoons apple juice concentrate
1 cup low-fat milk or low-fat soy
    milk

Preheat oven to 180°C.

Sift dry ingredients twice into a large
bowl. Add pumpkin and toss in flour
to coat well. Add yoghurt, lemon juice
and apple juice concentrate. Use a
knife to mix together. Slowly add
milk, still using a knife to bind
ingredients. The mixture will be
slightly sticky.

Scrape from bowl onto a lightly
floured board. Knead gently: too much
kneading will make scones heavy. Cut
into desired shapes. Place on a non-
stick scone tray and bake for 10–15
minutes.

APRICOT, BANANA AND APPLE MUFFINS

Makes 12

1 cup unbleached wholemeal plain flour

1 cup unbleached white plain flour

2 teaspoons baking powder

250 g fruit, freshly chopped (equal quantities of banana, apricot, apple, approximately pea size)

½ cup apple juice concentrate

2 tablespoons cold pressed grapeseed oil

¼ cup non-fat buttermilk

2 egg whites

Preheat oven to 180°C.

Sift dry ingredients twice into a large bowl. Add fruit and toss in flour to coat. Combine apple juice concentrate, oil and non-fat buttermilk. Add to flour and fruit and mix well. Beat egg whites until stiff peaks form and fold through the mixture. Spoon into a lightly greased muffin tray. Bake for 20–25 minutes.

BANANA CAROB MUFFINS

Makes 12

1¾ cups unbleached wholemeal plain flour

3 tablespoons carob powder

3 teaspoons baking powder

1 teaspoon cinnamon

1 teaspoon mixed spice

1 cup mashed banana

½ cup apple juice concentrate

¼ cup cold pressed grapeseed oil

¼ cup non-fat yoghurt

2 teaspoons vanilla essence

3 egg whites

Topping

2 heaped tablespoons rolled oats

½ teaspoon cinnamon

1 tablespoon apple juice concentrate

Preheat oven to 180°C.

Sift dry ingredients twice into a large bowl. Combine banana, apple juice concentrate, oil, yoghurt and vanilla. Add to flour and beat well. Beat egg whites until stiff peaks form. Fold in egg whites. Spoon into a lightly greased and floured muffin tray.

Add cinnamon to rolled oats. Sprinkle over top of each muffin. Add just a drop of the apple juice concentrate. Bake for 20–25 minutes.

BANANA AND CINNAMON MUFFINS

Makes 12

1 cup unbleached wholemeal plain
  flour
1 cup unbleached white plain flour
2 teaspoons baking powder
1 teaspoon cinnamon
½ teaspoon nutmeg
200 g banana, freshly chopped
  (approximately pea size)
½ cup apple juice concentrate
2 teaspoons vanilla essence
¼ cup cold pressed grapeseed oil
¼ cup non-fat buttermilk
2 egg whites
2 tablespoons rolled oats
extra cinnamon

Preheat oven to 180°C.

Sift dry ingredients twice into a large
bowl. Add banana and toss in flour to
coat well. Combine apple juice
concentrate, vanilla, oil and
buttermilk. Add to flour mixture and
mix well. Beat egg whites until stiff
peaks form. Fold through. Spoon into
a lightly greased muffin tray. Sprinkle
with rolled oats and extra cinnamon.
Bake for 20–25 minutes.

BLUEBERRY MUFFINS

Makes approximately 12 large muffins

2 cups unbleached wholemeal plain
  flour
2 teaspoons baking powder
200 g fresh blueberries
¼ cup cold pressed grapeseed oil
½ cup apple juice concentrate
¼ cup non-fat yoghurt
2 teaspoons vanilla essence
2 egg whites

Preheat oven to 180°C.

Sift flour and baking powder twice
into a large bowl. Add blueberries and
coat well with flour. Mix together oil,
apple juice concentrate, yoghurt and
vanilla. Make a well in the centre of
the flour and pour in half the liquid
mixture. Gently combine without
squashing blueberries. Add remaining
liquid.

Beat egg whites until stiff. Gently fold
egg whites through the blueberry
mixture until just combined. Spoon
mixture into a lightly oiled muffin
tray. Bake for 25–30 minutes. Remove
from oven.

These are deliciously moist muffins
that are best eaten warm from the
oven, without adding any spreads.

BROCCOLI AND CAULIFLOWER MUFFINS

Makes approximately 12 large muffins
200 g broccoli florets
200 g cauliflower florets
1 cup unbleached wholemeal plain flour
1 cup unbleached white plain flour
6 teaspoons baking powder
1 teaspoon nutmeg
2 cups oat bran
1 teaspoon grated Parmesan cheese
1¼ cups evaporated skim milk
½ cup cold pressed grapeseed oil
¼ cup apple juice concentrate
4 egg whites

Preheat oven to 180°C.

Steam broccoli and cauliflower until just tender and then plunge into cold water. Drain well.

Sift flour, baking powder and spice over cheese and oat bran in a large bowl. Add broccoli and cauliflower and toss through the flour to coat well. Combine milk, oil and apple juice concentrate and add to flour and oat mixture. Be careful not to break up cauliflower and broccoli pieces. Beat egg whites until stiff peaks form, and fold gently through the mixture.

Spoon into a lightly oiled and oat branned muffin tray. Bake for 25–30 minutes. Remove from muffin tray and place on a wire rack to cool. Cover with a tea towel.

FRESH PEAR AND CINNAMON MUFFINS

Makes approximately 12 large muffins

1 cup rolled oats

2 cups oat bran

1 cup unbleached white plain flour

6 teaspoons baking powder

3 teaspoons cinnamon

¼ cup lemon juice

¾ cup unsweetened orange juice

½ cup apple juice concentrate

½ cup cold pressed grapeseed oil

2 teaspoons vanilla essence

400 g Packham pears, cored and
    diced

3 egg whites

Preheat oven to 180°C.

Combine rolled oats and oat bran in a
bowl. Sift the flour, baking powder
and cinnamon over the oats and
combine.

Combine the lemon and orange juice,
apple concentrate, oil, vanilla and
pears in a large bowl. Slowly fold in
the dry ingredients, mixing well until
everything is combined. Beat the egg
whites until stiff peaks form and gently
fold through.

Spoon into a lightly oiled and oat
branned muffin tray. The mixture will
come up over the top of the tray.
Bake for 25–30 minutes. Remove from
muffin tray and place on a wire rack
to cool. Cover with a tea towel.

CARROT AND PINEAPPLE MUFFINS

Makes approximately 12 large muffins

1 cup unbleached wholemeal plain
   flour
1 cup unbleached white plain flour
2½ teaspoons baking powder
1 teaspoon mixed spice or ½ teaspoon
   nutmeg and ½ teaspoon cinnamon
100 g carrot, finely grated
100 g fresh pineapple, finely chopped
   (if using tinned pineapple make
   sure it has no added sugar and
   drain it well)
½ cup raisins, finely chopped
½ cup apple juice concentrate
⅓ cup non-fat buttermilk
2 teaspoons vanilla essence
¼ cup cold pressed grapeseed oil
2 egg whites

Preheat oven to 180°C.

Sift dry ingredients twice into a large
bowl. Add carrot, pineapple and
raisins and coat well with flour.
Combine apple juice concentrate,
buttermilk, vanilla and oil. Add to
flour mixture and mix well. Beat egg
whites until stiff peaks form. Fold
through the mixture.

Spoon into a muffin tray and bake for
20–25 minutes.

RHUBARB AND CINNAMON MUFFINS

Makes approximately 12 large muffins

1 cup rolled oats
2 cups oat bran
1 cup unbleached white plain flour
6 teaspoons baking powder
1 teaspoon baking soda
2 teaspoons cinnamon
400 g fresh rhubarb, chopped into
   small pieces
½ cup cold pressed grapeseed oil
½ cup apple juice concentrate
1 cup evaporated skim milk
2 teaspoons vanilla essence
4 egg whites

Preheat oven to 180°C.

Combine the rolled oats and oat bran
in a large bowl. Sift the next four
ingredients over the oats and mix
through. Add rhubarb and coat well
with flour.

Combine the oil, apple concentrate,
milk and vanilla and add to flour and
oat mixture. Beat egg whites until stiff
peaks form and gently fold through
the mixture.

Spoon into lightly oiled and oat branned muffin tray. Bake for 25–30 minutes. Remove from muffin tray and place on a wire rack to cool. Cover with a tea towel.

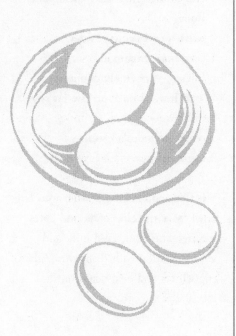

SPINACH AND CHEESE MUFFINS

Makes 12

1 cup unbleached wholemeal plain flour
1 cup unbleached white plain flour
2 teaspoons baking powder
1 teaspoon nutmeg
100 g fresh spinach, very finely chopped by hand
½ cup very finely grated low-fat grating cheese
½ cup evaporated skim milk
½ cup non-fat yoghurt
2 tablespoons apple juice concentrate
2 egg whites

Preheat oven to 180°C.

Sift dry ingredients twice in a large bowl. Add spinach and cheese and coat lightly with the flour. Combine milk, yoghurt and apple juice concentrate. Add to flour and spinach and mix well. Beat egg whites until stiff peaks form and fold through mixture.

Spoon into a lightly greased muffin tray. Bake for 25 minutes.

PLAIN PIKELETS

Makes approximately 15

½ cup unbleached white self-raising
  flour
½ cup unbleached wholemeal plain
  flour
½ cup low-fat milk or low-fat soy
  milk
1 teaspoon vanilla essence
2 egg whites
1 egg yolk

Sift flours into a large bowl. Add milk
and vanilla and beat to make a
smooth batter. Beat egg whites and
egg yolk and fold into the mixture.

Place dessertspoonfuls of mixture onto
a lightly greased hot pan. As bubbles
appear on top of pikelets quickly turn
over. Cook until both sides are nicely
browned.

Top with sliced tomato, low-fat
cheese, cottage cheese and herbs,
sugar-free jam or mashed banana.

DATE AND CINNAMON PIKELETS

Makes approximately 15

1 cup unbleached wholemeal plain
  flour
2 teaspoons baking powder
1 teaspoon cinnamon
10 dates, very finely chopped
½ cup low-fat milk or low-fat soy
  milk
1 teaspoon vanilla essence
2 egg whites

Sift flour and baking powder into large
bowl. Mix the cinnamon and dates
through the flour. Add milk and
vanilla and beat until smooth. Add
egg whites and beat again until
mixture is smooth.

Place dessertspoonfuls of mixture on a
lightly greased hot pan. As bubbles
appear on top of pikelets quickly turn
over and cook until both sides are
nicely browned.

INDEX